The Streetcar to LIFE

Copyright © 2025 by Bushel & Peck Books.
© First published in Italy by Piemme - Mondadori Libri S.p.A. in 2023.

This edition is published in arrangement with Grandi & Associati.

All rights reserved.

No portion of this book may be reproduced in any form without written permission from the publisher or author, except as permitted by U.S. copyright law.

Published by Milk & Cookies, an imprint of Bushel & Peck Books. Bushel & Peck Books is a family-run publishing house in Fresno, California, that believes in uplifting children with the highest standards of art, music, literature, and ideas. Find beautiful books for gifted young minds at www.bushelandpeckbooks.com.

This is a work of fiction. The story, all names, characters, and incidents portrayed in this production are fictitious. No identification with actual persons (living or deceased), places, buildings, and products is intended or should be inferred.

Type set in ImaginaryFriend BB and SchoolBook.
Designed by Lewis White.
Edited by Carol Lynch Williams.

Bushel & Peck Books is dedicated to fighting illiteracy all over the world. For every book we sell, we donate one to a child in need—book for book. To nominate a school or an organization to receive free books, please visit www.bushelandpeckbooks.com.

LCCN: 2024943999
ISBN: 978-1-63819-310-4

First Edition

Printed in the United States

1 3 5 7 9 10 8 6 4 2

The Streetcar to LIFE

The INSPIRING TRUE STORY
of EMANUELE DI PORTO

TEA RANNO

MILK &
COOKIES

FOREWORD

My name is Emanuele Di Porto and I am ninety-one years old. On the morning of October 16, 1943, when I was twelve, the Germans raided the Rome ghetto. My mother was taken and put on a truck. I ran into the street to save her, but instead she saved me.
I have told my story for more than seventy years. It's only recently gained popularity. People now recognize me on the street. They call me the kid who rode the tram. "The tram kid."
But I have never been a kid. At that time there was utter poverty. Everyone had to hurry to grow up and help their family.
I have never been a kid, but I will never be old, because in my heart, time has stopped. My story is captured in this book, with some parts being completely true, and others embellished by Tea to bring the past to life.

CHAPTER ONE

Gunshots jolt me awake in the dark night. I open my eyes and I'm disoriented. Mom is already up, looking out the window.

"Are the Germans there?" Betta asks from the bed next to mine.

Mom stays silent. She keeps looking out on the street to see what's happening. Via della Reginella, however, remains empty. She opens the shutters more, leans out to see to the end of the street, especially on the side of the Portico d'Ottavia. It's raining, and the streetlamp makes the raindrops on her hair sparkle like tiny fires. I gaze at her. She is beautiful.

"The Germans?" Betta asks again. She's the oldest of the girls and acts as if she's a mother.

"No," Mom says. "There's no one."

More gunshots break the silence, short and close bursts that could seem like firecrackers, except we're at war, and no one is celebrating with fireworks.

Mom steps back, closing the shutters. "They're far away," she whispers. "Don't be scared."

The shots seem to come from the Lungotevere.

"Probably someone playing a shooting game." She tries to make a joke, but her voice trembles. "Let's go back to sleep, it's still early."

She walks by the bed I share with my brother. He's complaining a bit.

"Does it hurt you?" she asks him, worried.

Nando looks at her without answering.

She places her hand on his forehead, as if checking for a fever, but there's no fever to be found, just her gentle touch.

"We'll go to the hospital later," she says. I can tell by the way she bites her lip that she wants to say something else. She would like to hold him close and comfort him like a baby, but she doesn't. Nando is fourteen. He's almost a man. You can't pick up an almost-man.

Since he's been sick, Nando's become like a little boy. Mom gives him another gentle touch and tells him the hospital will give him medicine to relieve his pain.

I want her comforting touch on my forehead. For her to be worried about me. I want her to call me "Mom's beauty," to hug me and make me feel special.

But I'm in good health.

Nando, on the other hand, has been suffering a lot lately and it breaks our mother's heart.

One day they brought him home from school. He was whiter than a rag and as cold as ice. Mom made him lie down on the bed. She covered him with all the blankets in the house. Then she massaged his legs and arms until he regained his color.

With Nando being sick, those of us who are healthy are invisible to her. Sometimes she looks at him with a dazed expression. It's like she's trying to figure out how she could stitch together a new body for him. One without sickness.

Mom is skilled with a needle and thread. She can make repairs that you can't see. When she uses her Singer sewing machine, you can be sure that the hem of the pants will be perfectly straight.

Now she returns to the window.

The gunfire keeps going. They patrol the borders of the ghetto like a belt, a fence that confines us in fear.

"Stay at home," they seem to say, "if you don't want to end up killed."

I huddle under the blankets, not because it's cold (it's still October and the weather is nice), but because my heart is racing.

Yesterday we saw a film at the cinema to take our

minds off things. It's called *Fuga a due voci*. There's a chance we'll go see it again.

"Con te, soli soli nella notte..." Gino Bechi, who played the lead, sang.

Mom sang along. She loves cinema because, she says, in that world of fantasy, nothing bad can happen. She can escape for a few hours of happiness.

Whenever Mom can set aside seven lire (one for each of us and one for her), we go to the Piazza del Gesù, to Centrale, and spend all afternoon.

"Remember, watch it twice!" says Dad. He doesn't come to the cinema.

Mom always lowers her head and smiles, even though the times are bleak.

I'm like her. I never get down. I know we're poor, there's war, hunger, and everything else, but you can't always be hopeless!

My motto is "Every man for himself," and imagination is a good way to save yourself. It always helps you find an escape route. If you get something nice, take it. That way you live better.

Last night, when we got home, Mom hummed while she made the most delicious cacio e pepe. I hid behind the door and watched her.

She's so beautiful. Her bangs fell in her eyes. Her long hair stopped on the neck, pinned with the hairpins. She was beautiful even after she cut her hair short like a man. All six of us kids were trembling because we thought Dad would be angry. Women with lipstick, polished nails, or trendy hairstyles are not seen as serious. But Dad didn't even notice.

Mom grated the cheese and sang. "Con te, sotto il raggio della luna…" When the others arrived, she stopped. War is war. Singing is not appropriate during war times.

I am lost in remembering. Then I hear it. Via della Reginella is bustling with people.

The sound of heels striking the cobblestones. Doors being knocked with the butt of a rifle. Orders being barked in German fill the air.

"They're taking away the men!" My mother almost cries out, then immediately lowers her voice. "I'm going to Termini, to warn Dad to stay down there. It's too dangerous here. If they see him, they'll take him."

It's true. Danger has emerged like a wolf from its lair. The previous calm was just a trap being set.

"I'll go and come back," she says, throwing a jacket over her shoulders. "Make sure you stay here. Don't move!"

"Can I come with you?" I ask. I'm big enough. If anything happens, I can defend her.

But she's already in the other room, where my uncles and cousins are sleeping. She reaches the door and pulls it shut with a thud that makes me shiver. With the Germans outside, any sound could spell trouble.

I seem to hear her running down the steps, but I'm guessing. The walls are thick and she has a light step.

Moving to the window, I look out.

Rain pours down. Via della Reginella is almost dark. The streetlights provide only a little light, making the road look slick and slippery. In front of Settimia's house there are soldiers with some papers in hand.

The lists! I think, and I feel a terrible anger.

A few weeks ago, the Germans demanded the Jews here in the Rome ghetto give fifty kilos of gold as a ransom for peace.

The commanding colonel, Kappler, threatened us. If the ransom wasn't paid, two hundred men would be taken to Germany to fight at the Russian border and ultimately meet their deaths.

We had to gather fifty kilos of gold.

How could that be collected in one day? Impossible! How do you find so much wealth in a time of extreme poverty?

Everyone did their best. They brought necklaces, bracelets, rings.

The Catholics helped us. "It's inhumane," they

said, "to put a bounty on the heads of people who must pay to stay alive."

In the end, we did it.

So, what do they want now?

Mom slips out the door, leans against the wall, and blends into the darkness. She's stealthy, moving like a shadow, unnoticed. My heart races as I watch her.

Piazza delle Tartarughe swarms with soldiers. Some hold papers. Others brandish guns. They intimidate the frightened people they've dragged out into the street.

"What do you want from us?" someone asks.

"Why are you grabbing us?" asks another.

But the soldiers don't answer. Instead they are forcing people. Yanking on them. Gesturing for them to move.

"Right now! Hurry up!" the soldiers yell. They're shoving people toward a waiting truck.

I can see part of the back of it from up here.

Other soldiers with clubs smash windows, break down doors, and try to pry open shutters.

There are people on the rooftops. They move stealthily, seeking safety. Two women leap from their windows to the courtyards below. Are they insane? They're risking their lives!

Mom, though, walks normally. She's not moving slowly or quickly. Thankfully no one notices her.

She takes the road toward Torre Argentina.

I can breathe again.

"Let's get dressed," says Betta.

In the darkness, we follow her command.

She gets Gemma dressed, too. My youngest sister understands we are in danger and remains quiet.

I quickly put on a shirt, socks, and shorts. On some freezing winter days, my legs turn purple, but I don't care.

From the street out front a woman screams, "Where are you taking us?"

I hurry to the window. Look out.

She's young and has a baby at her breast. The street's too dark to make out her face. She's unwilling to move forward. A soldier shoves her and she falls.

The baby begins to cry, and the soldier grabs the child by the neck, ready to throw him against the wall.

But the mother gets up and takes her baby. "It's nothing," I hear her say in a hushed voice. "Come on, my beautiful one. Come on. Be quiet."

There are others who shout, asking questions of those who speak only German and get angry because no one does what they say.

A man dressed in pajamas steps forward. He acts as a translator. "They're saying the men will be taken to labor camps and the women are to clean houses. The elderly and sick must also go. They say there's a medical center at the camp and they will receive care."

He stops for a moment, listens to the words of an officer, and translates again. "It's a temporary solution, they say. It will last until they win the war. Then we'll go back to our former lives."

It's a huge lie, but I can see everyone tries to believe it at the moment.

I look away.

No one has busted down our door. No one has told us to gather our belongings and follow them.

"Maybe we're not on the list," I say.

Betta walks over to where I am. She looks down at the street. "Maybe," she says, whispering. "As soon as Mom comes back, we'll escape."

My brothers go back to bed and Betta settles down next to Gemma.

I stay behind the shutters, thinking about Mom's journey. She has to travel from Turtle Square, down Via Paganica, until she reaches Torre Argentina and boards the bus at the station.

"Remember," she told me the first time she sent me to Termini alone, "the line is called MB. Make sure to read at the top, MB, which stands for Macao-Borgo."

The MB is the line that runs through the station all the way to the Vatican.

Minutes go by and she's still nowhere to be seen. Is she purposely avoiding coming back from Turtle Square, now overflowing with Germans? Or is she at Portico d'Ottavia instead? I strain my neck trying to get a better view, but all I see are SS troops and groups of people being herded along.

The dresser clock reads 5:25.

It's still dark outside, with rain pouring down. The soldier's helmets gleam in the wet. Children are crying and calling out for their mothers. The soldiers shout even louder.

I feel like I'm in a nightmare. Until yesterday we believed we were safe. We thought the Germans would keep their word and honor the agreements. Now, instead, only lies.

It's fortunate Dad went to work today even though it's a Saturday. Saturdays are usually a day of rest for Jews. It's why the Germans found everyone at home.

Dad believes in respecting the day of rest because God commanded it. But when the family is in need, Dad says, God doesn't take offense if you go to earn a few cents to buy the bread and food you need to feed them.

He's a street vendor. He sells souvenirs to both the Germans who arrive at the station with the convoys and the soldiers who come from the front. He sells postcards, combs, wallets, and keychains. The trains mostly arrive at night and so he goes to work at night. He comes home around noon. Mom keeps watch at the window. If he signals to her from the street that he hasn't made a single penny that day, she'll borrow money from a neighbor to put food on the table.

Here, everyone does so, at least to make up for lunch. In the evening we often go to bed with an empty stomach. Sometimes we eat just a potato or a piece of bread.

The worst part is that with three families sharing this house, sometimes one may have food while the others don't. There are those who eat and those who watch you eat and the food sticks in your throat.

But it's the war. A black misery makes these terrible things happen.

It was three in the morning when Dad got up. His belt dropped and made a clanging noise. It sounded like a coin bouncing on the floor. I woke up and called to him.

"Go to sleep, Emanuele," he said. "It's still early."

A small amount of light seeped through the shutters. I watched him putting on his pants and shirt. He washed his face with the basin water. Then he took his cap and said to Mom, "Ginotta, I'm going."

He spoke softly, so as not to wake up the children. If the youngest one was awakened, he wouldn't stop crying.

Mom's name is Virginia. Virginia Piazza. Within the family, though, she's referred to as Ginotta.

After Dad left, I struggled to fall asleep. Not because of the noise. At three in the morning, the Germans hadn't begun firing, and Via della Reginella was silent as it could be with all the residents asleep.

It seemed like any other night.

I thought about the movie and the song's lyrics and envisioned myself in the dark with Ester. But it was better not to think of that. She's rich and I'm poor and between rich and poor things can't work, Mom says.

However, anything is possible in a fantasy. I kept imagining myself holding her hand and walking with her to find a place of refuge.

CHAPTER TWO

I continued to peer through the slats of the shutters. Outside is full of people now. I'm glad Mom went out when the street was less congested.

The sky is still dark. A heavy rain still falls. The ground is flooded, and the German boots kick up water and mud on those who have been taken from their beds. They're trying to find shelter as best they can.

"I want Mom," Gemma says.

Betta embraces her. "She'll be here soon."

"When?"

"In time to tell Dad."

"When?" Gemma asks again.

"In a bit."

Gemma twists a finger in her hair, then starts crying. Betta gives her a crust of bread. "Eat, come on, Gemma."

The room goes silent, but downstairs is a hub of

noise and activity. I look at the square again.

"Don't lean out," Betta says to me. "They can see you."

"The shutters are closed," I say.

I can't wait for Mom to return, to be safe here with us.

A soldier reads out names. It feels like we're in school, during attendance. But this is an attendance that chills the blood.

In recent days, rumors have circulated throughout the ghetto about lists containing the names of Jewish families to be deported.

At first, I didn't believe it was true. It seemed like foolishness. Something said just to scare us.

But there are lists!

Here's the reason I didn't believe the rumors. I've come to know the Germans. Not all of them are bad people.

I sell combs just like my dad does. And wallets and elastic bands. I sell to German people at the station, earning money that helps my family.

Sometimes they give me bread or canned meat. There's one man who always smiles at me and buys the elastic band even if he doesn't need it.

After September 8, though, when Italy signed an armistice with the Allies, things changed. The Italians became enemies and Jews were doubly targeted for being both Italian and Jewish.

If Grandma were still alive, she would say this was the fate of our people, to be persecuted. I refuse this fate, though. I don't want a destiny of persecution. I don't want to be treated differently from other Italians just because I don't believe Jesus Christ is the son of God.

How much longer will Mom be? She'll be all wet. She didn't even take an umbrella, as if she doesn't care about the rain, but she could catch pneumonia.

I almost go down to look for her.

But no. She said not to move. To wait for her here. And besides, at this moment, I'm the head of the family. Dad isn't here. Nando is ill and doesn't count. I'm twelve years old and for four years I've been earning bread for myself and for the others.

I watch as the Germans round up people with suitcases. They load them onto the truck not caring who they are. Not only men, but also women and children. And old people. What will they do with the old in the labor camps? Some of them aren't even good for lifting a stick, let alone working with a hoe! If the Germans leave the older people at home, they'll save money.

"They're taking everyone away," Betta says into my ear. Her voice is filled with disbelief.

Gemma starts to cry again, left alone in bed.

"Go to her," I say. My heart pounds. It beats so loud it feels like it's drowning out all other sounds.

Mom is gone.

Maybe she's decided not to come back. Or maybe Dad convinced her to go with him to Testaccio. They know we can handle it, staying here without them. We have aunts and uncles in the other rooms. Those who are really in danger are Mom and Dad, who are out on the street.

It's better for you and Dad to go see the relatives in Testaccio. Yes, I think.

"Shall we go?" asks Betta.

"No. Mom said to stay here. To wait for her."

The rain comes down harder. The cobblestones are shiny and slippery-looking. I've fallen here before, and it almost cost me my life.

It was raining like this, and I was getting water from the fountain when I fell and the jar broke. It cut me from my armpit almost to my elbow. I was taken to the hospital to be stitched up.

When I got there it seemed like I was entering the Grand Hotel. The bed was clean. The room was heated. There was food and drink. I couldn't believe it.

Two days later, when I was discharged, I almost wished I hadn't been.

Mom was still worried, and she took care of me like she's now taking care of Nando. Her concern for him will last a lifetime because his illness will never go away. We'll always feel guilty for our healthy bodies.

The silence in our rooms is deafening. No noises or voices can be heard even though there are twenty people in the house. Fear has quieted everyone, or they're speaking in hushed tones so that the words can't be heard.

Waiting at the window was a terrible idea. Time seems to stand still.

The scolding from Mom when I arrived late in the dark one night is still fresh in my mind: she blamed me. I didn't understand why. I didn't stay out all night!

"I've been waiting for you for two hours!" she said, furious, when I got home. All that for being two hours late. Now I understand how she felt. Every minute seems to last a hundred years.

The situation down below has become even more hostile. Maybe it's because higher-ups have come and the soldiers want to make a good impression. They shout louder and push people with their rifles. Pieces of paper, some pieces of glass, something that might be a doll (you can't see it well from up here), and a broken umbrella are scattered in the street. The rain falls straight into the puddles.

Mom doesn't have an umbrella. If she doesn't

come soon to dry off, she'll catch pneumonia, I think.

"Manue," says Betta. "Can you see her?"

I shake my head no. I lean a little closer to the window. Then ...

"There she is!" I say. My heart jumps in my chest with excitement.

Careful, Ginotta, careful!

She walks normally, as if it is a market day and she's coming back with the shopping bag. Mom crosses the square and heads towards the entrance of Via della Reginella.

A soldier stops her, grabs her arm, and tries to drag her toward the truck despite her attempts to resist.

Mom!

Then I shout. "Mommaaa!" I break away from my sister and sprint down the stairs, pushing past anyone in my way. I reach the truck.

My mother is there, guarded by the German.

"Resciùd," she says between her teeth without looking at me "Resciùd! Go away. Escape!"

I shake my head, stay there, staring, immobile, at her and the soldier.

"Resciùd!" She looks pained and angry. She motions for me to run. "Go, obey!"

The German grabs me by the arm and throws me onto the truck.

My mother is furious. She can't calm down, and

she looks at her friend Settimia, who has also been taken along with her mother and sisters.

She mutters under her breath, "He had to stick his nose into it. I told him. I told him."

Then she says to me, "I told you. I told you. You should have stayed at home. Not come down here."

Next to her is a woman with a baby at her breast. The German who took me looks at her and she covers herself with a handkerchief.

My mother doesn't give up. She speaks to the soldier. She says, "Nicht iud, nicht iud!" and points at me. He's not a Jew, he's not a Jew!

He does not believe it. He looks at me. Looks at her. Sees that we look alike. Orders her to be quiet, and since he has the rifle in his hand, I tremble at the thought that he might shoot her.

She calms down but whispers between her teeth, "He wanted to get caught. I told him to stay at home. I told him." She doesn't look at me. She treats me as if she doesn't know me.

There's a loud noise from Via dei Funari and the German turns. My mother takes advantage of the moment and manages to throw me out of the truck.

I find myself in the square, surrounded by soldiers. In my mind her voice commands, "Resciùd!"

I don't dare look back at her, but I feel her eyes on me, pushing me to go.

"Away from here, run!"

This time I obey, not wanting to anger her further.

Going back home is not an option, as I would have to pass the truck and the soldier who took me, risking being caught again. I walk slowly, trying to blend in with the crowd and not draw attention to myself. My hands are in my pockets and my shoulders are stooped. I keep my gaze on the ground. The rain soaks me. My feet are wet in my cloth shoes, causing a chill to run through my body.

I walk down Via di Sant'Ambrogio, a narrow and almost-dark street.

The Germans are too busy rounding up people from the other streets to notice me. I walk as if I'm going to buy milk. My throat is tight and my hands are still in my pockets.

I hug the wall just as my mother did before. From open windows I can hear voices and cries, orders to hurry, and the sound of breaking glass, cutlery falling, and doors being knocked down with rifle butts.

Via di Sant'Ambrogio is almost empty now. Soldiers are busy getting people out of their homes. They don't pay any attention to me.

"Raus!" they shout. "Raus, raus! "

I move faster and pass by Anna's house, Betta's friend who loves me like a brother. The house is wide open and empty. I think of Anna in the hands of the SS and my heart aches even more.

"Resciùd," mother's voice commands in my mind. I go straight ahead without turning back.

Not even thirty feet ahead, a soldier with a submachine gun appears. I retreat like a crab, crawling against the wall until I find a recessed area. I hide in the darkness hardly breathing.

Not too far away is Erminia's house. She owns a cow. When she can, Mom sends me to Erminia with a few cents and the bottle to fill with milk.

The cow is awake now and complains loudly, as if she understands the tragedy that's happening to us.

The German stops. Maybe he can't believe there's a real cow in a city house.

I'm sweating. I suck in my stomach. Close my eyes. Repeat my mother's name in my mind. *Ginotta. Ginotta. Ginotta.* I say it as if this is a prayer.

The soldier walks past without seeing me. I wait for him to pass, then leave my hiding place and hurry on this road that's too narrow to be safe.

Now there's more of a crowd in front of Portico d'Ottavia. Voices rise, calling out names. Next to the excavations is a second box truck where entire families are being loaded.

How many people are escaping? Have any Catholics opened their doors to hide someone? Are there others like me who are taking advantage of the confusion to disappear? I only know that the truck is already full of women, children, and the elderly.

Franco's grandfather is lifted from his wheelchair and thrown into the crowd where Anna and her brother Luigi stand out. I hope they don't see me or recognize me because if they call out, the Germans will catch me. I'll end up on the truck too. That can't happen, not after Mother risked her life to save mine.

I walk. Head down, hands in my pockets, rain pouring from my hair down my face, back, and legs. I feel nothing. I see nothing. Just the road now and my feet moving on their own. One step and another and another.

I think of my mother.

She's too smart to not jump off the truck. Maybe, at this moment, she's walking slowly to get away from the ghetto. Maybe she's slipped into some alley, into some basement where she found others like us hiding.

Maybe she's heading toward Campo de' Fiori or Torre Argentina. Or maybe she's gone down into the basement of the Mattei building. We took refuge there during the bombing of San Lorenzo. Everything was shaking and it seemed like the end of the world.

I think of Mom and tell myself that she gave me life twice. When she gave birth to me and when she threw me off the truck.

I feel like crying, but I don't, because I'm not a little boy. Mother is counting on me and I can't let her down. Crying wastes time and I have to hurry.

I reach the Monte Savello terminus and the tram is about to leave. I get on. I approach the ticket collector.

"I'm Jewish," I whisper. "The Germans are looking for me."

He doesn't waste time even looking at me. He says, "Come here, next to me. Don't move!"

And so I do what he says.

The tram leaves, and I know nothing more about my mother or the others.

CHAPTER THREE

The sky is dark. It's still raining. The tram feels like a piece of day moving through the night.

The ticket collector doesn't look at me. He pretends he doesn't know me. Occasionally, though, he turns toward me to make sure I'm there.

Yes, I'm here. Where would I go?

I curl up on the seat. Bring my knees to my chest. Hug them. I close my eyes. I feel like hugging Mom. I want to feel her smooth skin, her dress that smells of apples. She hides the apples in the wardrobe and takes them out on days when I'm too hungry.

My shoes leave traces of mud on the seat. It dries and comes off like dust. With my eyes closed, I keep thinking about Mom. I see her in the truck and I want to shout, "Run, Ginotta, run! Resciùd!" but my voice doesn't come out. It seems dead inside my throat.

I rest my chin on my knees. The tram is moving. People are getting on, getting off. Voices are quiet.

These are not all Jews, I think.

"Jews can never feel safe," said Grandmother. She immediately started the persecution story that I didn't want to hear. I can't stand tragedies and I try to find a reason for happiness in every day.

But now, after what's happened in the ghetto, I realize Grandmother was right. We are a persecuted people. We're never really safe. Because at any moment—at any moment—someone can come and chase us out of where we are and send us to our death.

The tram brakes with a jolt that almost makes me fall. I grab on to the support. Put my feet on the ground to keep my balance. A van has cut us off. It's black and big and followed by four motorbikes.

"You little. . ." says the driver, cursing.

The man next to me looks like a professor. He says the Germans behave as if they were the masters of Rome. They allow themselves to do whatever they want in our house without anyone having the guts to stop them.

"Isn't that so?" he asks.

The few other travelers don't answer.

He sighs, pulls half an unlit cigar out of his pocket. He looks at it, twirls it between his fingers as if he doesn't know what to do with it, then puts the cigar back in his pocket.

He has a black beard, a dark tie under his brown

coat, a leather bag so full it looks as if it will split at any moment. I want to ask him if he knows how to stop the raid. If he knows someone who can stop the Germans and drive them out of the ghetto. Out of Rome. Out of Italy.

Our eyes meet. His are good. In mine, I know he reads fear. And because I don't want him to speak to me, to remember me, I turn to the window.

It's pouring. Some people have umbrellas. Others cover their heads with sacks or pieces of cardboard. The few military cars drive with their headlights on and their windshield wipers running, unable to clear the windows of water. The gutters float leaves, bits of wood, and a few bird feathers.

Germans are everywhere as black as cockroaches that have emerged from the sewers. I can't see the swastika on the helmet from here, but I know it's there. On the side, above the ear.

It's the sign I stared at when Mom said I wasn't a Jew. I had put myself in Jonàv's mouth. I looked at the swastika between the eagle's talons while Mom said "Resciùd!" and I couldn't move.

The tram stops. Some people get off, others get on. A wet smell comes from the street, even from clothes. From the bundles some people wear on their chests or under their arms.

One of those bundles moves, begins to cry. It's

not a bundle but an infant. The girl holding the baby is pale.

An old man gives up his seat to her. "Come, sit down," he tells her.

She shakes her head. "I'll get off at the next stop." She can't take a step because four fascists have come up. They scare you just to look at them.

She's Jewish like me, I think. My heart beats fast, as if I've run from Macao-Borgo to Termini without stopping. I feel it in my throat, in my belly, in my ears. It pounds through my body like a prisoner who wants to escape from a cage.

The fascists speak in whispers. The trousers of one rub against my leg. From their clothes comes the smell of soap and cigarettes. Their hair is sticky with grease.

"That's what happens when you betray the Germans," says the biggest with satisfaction. "That turnabout on September 8 made them angry, and now, with the traitors, they act like enemies. Can you see? They're rounding up all Rome. So in the meantime, they get rid of the Jews."

The old man looks at them as if he wants to set them on fire. Luckily, they don't notice. Sometimes just a glance is enough to send you to the prison on Via Tasso, where they torture you.

The skinny fascist says that Hitler and Mussolini

will take back Italy, that they will make an empire. He says the Allies aren't strong enough to defeat the German Wolf.

A kind of smile appears on the old man's lips. Again, the fascists don't notice. They go on talking about Mussolini and Hitler, of the Jews as if they were lice to get rid of.

"De-fi-ni-ti-va-men-te!" says the one with the mustache.

The girl with the baby clutches the child to her chest so hard she makes him cry again.

Now they'll ask for her papers and arrest her! I think, terrified.

The old man must think so too. He takes the baby and says, "Come here, bello de nonno." He's speaking to the newborn. "Who knows what your mother is thinking today." He turns to her and says, "Mari, wake up! Go, take these keys!"

He hands her a keyring with the Pope's medal on it. It's one of those sold on Sundays at St. Peter's during the blessing. Almost all Catholics have one, and this is enough to reassure the fascists, who disregard it, and go back to their talking.

The tram stops abruptly and the one with the mustache almost falls on top of me. As he straightens, he swears at the driver. "I'll make you lose your license."

The girl clutches at the tram handle to keep from falling. To the big guy who's bumped into her and then apologized, she replies by lowering her head.

The old man continues to play with the newborn. Tells him he's as beautiful as an angel. Indeed as beautiful as one of the cherubs in the painting of the Madonna at Santa Maria in Vallicella.

I look to the ground.

The boots of the fascists are black, shiny. The girl's shoes look like my mom's. The ticket collector's shoes are worn at the toe. The old man's shoes have laces. Who knows if Mom is still in Piazza delle Tartarughe?

When we reach Ponte Vittorio Emanuele, the old man gets up and says in a rude tone of voice, "Mari,' shall we be late again today? Let's go, come on!"

He grabs her by the arm, makes his way through the people, pulling her along with him.

I turn to the ticket collector. His face has no answers on it. Is he also thinking that the old man just saved a Jewess and her baby?

Rome is dark. Black, it seems, with pain and fear.

Trucks with gray tarps pass us. Others pull up beside us. We've stopped at a traffic light. In one truck, from the gap between the container and the tarpaulin, hands emerge. Desperate faces appear that someone from inside grabs hold of.

Tears drip from my eyes without me being able to stop them.

Maybe Mom is here, close to me. Maybe a German grabs her hair to pull her in. Maybe she's calling for help, and I, who is just a step away, can't hear her. Can't help her.

"Poor things," murmurs a woman who's all wet. Her teeth chatter with the cold.

"It's all an error," says a priest. "A mistake. They'll send them home. The Pope will certainly do something to prevent these infamities."

The truck full of Jews starts off again with a black gasp.

The tram also drives. It's slower and can't keep up. Through the gaps in the truck, hands drop tickets that catch the air.

Later I will learn that during the journey, Mom threw the bread cards and the cigarette she had in her pocket off the truck. On the envelope she wrote, "Do a good deed. Take these cards to the Di Porto family, in Via della Reginella."

The good work will be done. The cards will arrive at our house. They'll show that all Mom's thoughts were for us. They'll show that in the world there are also good people who don't take advantage of the misfortunes of others.

This will happen in a few days.

Now, I'm on the tram that takes me around Rome, while the raid continues in the ghetto.

"What? Are they taking the kids away too?" asks a stunned man who must have just heard the news. "What do they do with the kids? They send the men to work and the women to be servants, but kids?"

No one answers him.

Kids are useless, they're just mouths to feed, better to get rid of them, Mom must have thought. She did everything she could to save me.

I am reminded of the words that an old fascist said to a young fascist. "Remember that the children of enemies are equally enemies, even if they are little ones. When they grow up, they will kill you and your family, so they must be eliminated."

The thought makes me shiver.

The ticket collector looks at me. He sees the short pants, the lightweight shirt and, thinking I'm cold, takes off his scarf and spreads it over my shoulders. Then he goes back to tearing tickets and punching the season ticket cards with his pliers.

The Germans don't know that they would get a bargain with me. I've been bringing home the bacon and working better than a man since I was six years old. They check how tall you are. How thin you are. They think you're no good at anything and they get rid of you.

The scarf is blue and smells of camphor.

Blue like the sea of Ostia. Like my friend Attilio's jumper. Like an old wallet of Dad's that Mom gave me when I was little. She put a nickel in it. One day, while playing, I slipped the money through the keyhole of the house and there it remained.

CHAPTER FOUR

I lean my head against the glass and close my eyes.

I see Ginotta Piazza coming out of the gate, walking unnoticed.

I see her singing so she will be noticed.

I see her singing "Soli soli nella notte," as she grates the cheese, as she sets the table, while talking to Aunt Elena, while she moves the pedal of the Singer sewing machine and the trousers take shape, while she tells me to go to school because I have to learn to read and write so no one can trick me, while she gives me the ten lire that I need to buy second-hand items to resell in Campo de' Fiori.

I think of when there was the bombing in San Lorenzo and she took us to the shelter. Instead of staying in the shelter with us, Mom went back home to fix us something to eat.

She's brave. She's not afraid of anything. She's too smart to be fooled by four punches to the head that tear you away from your family and take you to some other home, where they make you work hard.

"Manue," she tells me, "take the pot, wrap it in the tablecloth, and bring it down."

I obey.

Every evening, weather permitting, we gather with the neighbors in front of the wine shop. We buy a liter, a liter and a half, then, sitting at the tables, we open the food bundles and eat. That's why they call us the fagottari—the bundle-bearers.

It's nice to eat out on the street with everybody. The adults drink wine and talk about weddings and engagements. About this one's bar mitzvah, that one's bat mitzvah, Sukkot, the Feast of Booths. All that talk drives us kids crazy, because building the booth, decorating it with fruit and vegetables, then living in it for eight days seems like a game.

On those evenings I always sit next to Attilio, who is fifteen years old. He's almost a man but unlike the other men here, he treats me as an equal. He knows a hundred things more than I do, because he likes to study and I don't. Because he reads books and newspapers and I don't. Because he is interested in politics and I'm not. Because. . .

A sharp pain in my foot almost makes me cry out.

I open my eyes wide. I look for Attilio, Mom, the pot, the wineglasses on the set table. Instead I find myself on the tram. My foot is under the boot of a painter who talks to another about the roundup.

"It's not only in the ghetto," he says. "It's a raid all over Rome. Even in Testaccio, in Borgo, in Garbatella."

"It's not true."

"It is. Believe me. They're taking away all the Jews, all of them. Really."

I hold on to the seat to avoid falling.

So, the Germans also took dads, uncles, and cousins who live in the other neighborhoods. It's not true that Rome's safe.

"What about the fifty kilos of gold that was supposed to be used for their ransom?" asks a man in a baker's apron.

"Yeeeees, sure! The fifty kilos of gold! They just stole it. They don't keep their word."

"But they promised."

"Who, the Germans? And you believe them?"

We all believed it. Handing over the gold, feeling safe. We didn't doubt. We didn't think it might be a trick. That it was a way of stripping ourselves of what we had left. And now they still take us away.

I bite my lip to keep from shouting that it was a betrayal, that the Germans set a trap for us.

The ticket collector tries to change the subject.

An old man on the other side of the tram shouts,

"If Pius XI were still alive, this kind of crap wouldn't have happened."

"Sure it wouldn't!" the worker says. "Jews are Jews and Catholics are Catholics. Each defends his own people!"

"That's not true, had he been alive. . ."

They interrupt him to argue. Who defends the new pope? He says he's a friend of Hitler.

Someone says if the pope were a real head of state, a real religious leader, he would have already done something, but instead? He shuts up, pretending not to see and not to hear.

The voices get louder, angrier.

The ticket collector struggles to calm the painter. They must be friends because he calls him by name and tells him to stop, please, that there is no need to make a fuss.

Then, looking at the others, the ticket collector says, "All I'm saying is that if any of us can do something, we must do it. If each of us, in our own small way, does something. . ." He stops talking.

I look out the window.

It's raining slow. It's raining tired. It's raining like tears on the face of this city.

This is my city even though I am Jewish. I was born here, my father and mother were born here. So were my grandparents, aunts, uncles, cousins. All the rest of the family.

This is where I feel at home.

"The pope," someone says.

"The old one?"

"No, the new one. The old has long since passed away, and the dead can't change the lives of the living."

The word *pope* reminds me of one of the stories that Lia tells. She's our upstairs neighbor who comes to warm herself by our fire in the evenings. It's a story about the priest.

One day he entered the shop of a Jewish woman and she gave him an umbrella for shelter. The priest said that he was passing through, that he didn't know when he would be able to return it.

"When you become pope," she said. This was like saying he could keep the umbrella. The priest left, and the woman forgot about him.

Many years later, she received a letter from the Vatican. "What does the Vatican want from me?" she said to herself. She couldn't believe it. The priest had become pope for real and wanted to return her umbrella.

"Who was that pope?" I once asked Lia.

"Pope Sixtus," she said.

I understood that it was a story, a made-up fact. The last Pope Sixtus lived in Rome four hundred years ago.

The men who are arguing get off the tram and peace returns. In my heart, however, there is war. If they are rounding up all Rome, it means that they are going house by house. They're pulling people out of their beds, closets, storage spaces, even from the chests full of water on the terrace, where occasionally someone hides.

"They are taking all of them." That's what the guy said.

All of us.

As if we are murderous criminals that need to be in prison or we'll destroy the world. I let out a sob I can't help and try to conceal it with a cough.

The ticket collector looks at me. I nod to indicate everything is fine.

However, the soldiers didn't come to our home. Nobody broke down the gates and doors. Nobody came to get us.

Or maybe they did. Maybe it happened after I left. Maybe right now Nando, Betta, Gioele, Beniamino, and Gemma are on a truck and at our home there is devastation.

Or maybe not. Maybe they're all still there. All safe.

A woman's voice breaks the silence. "The raid didn't start today, you know!" she says. She's angry. "The Jews have been deprived of rights since the time of the racial laws in 1938. And tell me, in your opinion, is a man without rights a man?"

No one answers.

"I'll tell you," she says. "No! A man without rights is something that anyone can do as they please with!"

I turn to look at her. She's a beautiful girl, with dark hair and dark eyes. She wears a green coat and has the attitude of a warrior.

The guy standing next to her tells her to shut up, that such talk is too dangerous. She doesn't care and keeps on talking. People look at her in amazement. She's truly crazy. She likes to take big risks!

"Things must be called by their proper names," she says. "The camps where they send trainloads of Jews are not work camps, but. . ."

I plug my ears.

I don't want to hear!

It's not true!

Mom is at home. The Germans didn't raid us. I'm going to Via Trionfale where people have money and give me better stuff to resell in Campo de' Fiori. They know me. I go under the windows and shout, "Women, the ragman has arrived! Money and rags, women!" There's always someone who gives me something.

The girl still talks about human rights and the laws that are wrong.

A tall man with a wooly hat on his bald head interrupts her. "If I were in your shoes, I would listen to the advice of friends and not speak out of turn," he says.

"Good thing you're not!"

He grimaces. "You women. Always meddling in other people's business. Leave politics to the men. Think instead of darning socks and keeping the house clean!"

The girl laughs. "I bet you know more about politics than Mussolini and Hitler combined."

"I bet you are Jewish."

"Maybe," she says. She looks at him still. "I, on the other hand, bet you are a Catholic."

"From head to toe!" he says, all swollen with pride.

"And that's a relief!" Without giving him time to respond she says, "Then you will, no doubt, know what 'You shall love your neighbor as yourself' means."

He's about to reply, but I see him reconsider. He closes his mouth and looks at her as if she's setting a trap for him.

"Who is your neighbor?" she asks.

The bald man keeps looking at her without answering.

"Everyone except Jews?" she asks. "Everyone except homosexuals? Or Gypsies? Or the Blacks?"

In the tram the silence is absolute. Everyone may still think she's crazy. I think she's insanely brave. At the next stop she gets off.

The silence continues even after she has gone.

CHAPTER FIVE

We arrive at Piazzale Flaminio. I'm so hungry.

It's about eight days before Easter, when you can't even touch a crumb of leavened bread. It's a real torment, especially in this time of starvation when bread is the only food you can get.

That's why we celebrate, at Easter, when with a ciriòla or a loaf in our hands. All of us boys and girls run through the ghetto shouting, "Bread again, everybody! Bread is back!"

I feel like I can actually smell the bread.

And not only that! I feel like I'm back in the days before the war, when Mom whipped twenty eggs making one of those omelets that could raise the dead.

I close my eyes to see her in the kitchen as she heats the oil and then throws in all those eggs to fry, seasoning them with cheese, garlic, and parsley. The smell is so strong that my mouth waters.

"Hey, little boy," the ticket collector says, shaking me. "Didn't you hear me?"

I turn and see that he's pulled a nicely greased cirióla from a wrapper. It's so stuffed it seems to have doubled in size.

"I'm talking to you, yes. What are you doing, sleeping? Aren't you hungry? Don't you like omelets with potatoes?" He doesn't wait for my answer. He splits it in two parts and hands me one. "Tie', eat," he says.

Half a ciriòla with a piece of potato omelet?

This is what I call a dream, I think. I don't reach out my hand for fear the bread and butter will disappear.

"Take it, come on! It's good! Trust me." He takes a bite from his part.

I don't make him say it again. I reach out my hand, say thank you, and eat. It's so good!

I eat slowly to make the half-loaf last as long as I can. The ticket collector, on the other hand, finishes his in four bites and goes back to taking the tickets.

After a while he hands me a bottle of water. "Drink, come on," he says.

I drink. I eat. I think of Mom who maybe is thirsty, maybe is hungry, and the bread turns bitter.

I also think of Dad. Who knows if he managed not to get caught.

Caught.

And the rest of my family?

Actually, I don't worry about them too much. I know Betta is taking care of them. She's clever and knows what to do in any situation.

The tram starts again.

People get on, get off, bump into each other, step on each other's toes, grumble, and argue like every day.

A terrible misfortune has happened in the ghetto, but in these other quarters of Rome life goes on as normal. Women have food to put on the table. Children play in the streets. Old men sit behind windows watching people go by, airplanes flying overhead reminding us the Allies are coming to Italy. They will liberate it completely.

The rain has stopped. The sun has come out, making the branches of the trees look darker.

At Piazza Fiume the tram makes a longer stop.

"How long before we leave again?" someone asks.

"Ten minutes," the ticket collector says. He looks at me. "Come, let's go pee. Don't you need to pee?"

I've been holding it for a long time.

"Let's get off the tram."

We do. We turn on a narrow street and come to a small garden.

"Go behind that bush," he says.

He picks another one and we lighten up.

This ticket collector is an angel sent from God. I hope God also sends an angel to my mother because she needs one more than I do.

When we get back on the tram, he adjusts my scarf, makes me sit in my usual seat, then asks the driver, "When do we leave?"

"Two minutes."

He leans out the door warning those in the lay, "We'll be gone in two minutes!"

We stop again at Monte Savello. The Germans are still here, loading people onto trucks. It is just past midday and they haven't finished yet. From Quattro Capi Bridge, I see another caravan arriving. Soldiers lead and follow it.

There's Samuel among them! My heart leaps. I know him well. We sometimes speak in his laboratory. He's a very good shoemaker, one who can make perfect soles and heels in a flash.

Quattro Capi Bridge connects the ghetto to Tiberina Island. But he lives in Via dei Funari. What's he doing there? He got away and they stopped him? Or maybe someone spied on him and the Germans ran to get him?

I watch my friend. He's dragging his leg, as if he's injured. He crosses the street, going with the others toward the Portico d'Ottavia. Then he disappears.

I may never see him again.

The Germans will take him to forced labor. They'll let him die of fatigue. He works hard with glue, tacks, hammer, and scissors. He's never held a hoe in his hand. Not even a rifle. Not a bomb.

They can't take him to the Russian border to defend Germany. He doesn't give a damn about the war. He's like me. We care only about being left alone, living with what little we have, without bothering anyone.

I cry then wipe away the tears.

No bad thoughts!

I'll find him again in the laboratory. He'll say to me, "Pass me the seed sowing!" And I'll hand him the small nails.

"Pass me the seedbed preparation!" And I'll bring that kind of screwdriver with a slit at the tip.

"Take that small knife there, help me iron this piece of leather."

The ticket collector puts his hand on my shoulder. "Don't move," he whispers.

I don't understand.

He glances at a small group of SS men standing around an officer. The officer looks toward us. He says something. Two soldiers break away from the group. They're coming to us.

I'm about to get up. The word *resciùd* screams in my head.

The ticket collector stops me.

"Don't move!" he says again, then wraps the scarf around my neck, half hiding my face.

The Germans walk quickly. One wears glasses The other has a bag hanging from his belt.

They're coming to pick me up. Someone has recognized me, mentioned my name. Now I will end up on the truck.

Mom's sacrifice was for nothing.

The ticket collector hands me the ticket punch for the cards. "Hold on a bit," he says.

The soldiers have their machine guns drawn. There's an air of hunting dogs searching for prey.

When they get close, it feels like an iron fist squeezes my stomach. With the ticket punch in my hand, I look at the ticket collector as if he were my father. He looks at me and hands me a pad.

"Lore'," he says. "Count how many are left. Don't make a mistake!"

For a long moment I feel as if I'm underwater. The noises disappear, the colors too. There's only a machine gun too close to my chest. The strap of a uniform too close to my face. A hand too close to my throat.

I don't know how long it lasts. I don't know if it's a few seconds or several minutes.

When I breathe again the soldiers have reached

two men sitting further ahead. "Documents!" says the one with the glasses.

The men obey, but they don't hurry. They're not Jews. They're not afraid. They show their papers to the Germans, who check them carefully before turning to the other passengers.

When they finish checking everyone's papers, they get off the tram. They're unhappy. It's like they didn't win a prize. They reach the officer and nod.

Are they looking for me? Has someone called on me?

I think of Mom and I feel as if I'm dying.

Even if she had papers in her pocket, what would she need them for? They say her name is Virginia Piazza, born in Rome in 1906, Jewish.

Breathing becomes more difficult. It's as if my throat has tightened. What would Attilio do if he were in my place?

You have to be a man, I imagine him saying to me.

I hand the ticket puncher back to the ticket collector, pull the scarf from my nose and mouth, and think about my job as a ragman.

Once I bought the jacket of a dead man from his widow for ten lire. I resold it for forty lire. A real bargain. I gave my mother twenty-eight, and I kept two for myself (one for ice cream and one for the cinema). Then I put ten aside to buy something to resell the next day.

Does that mean I'm a man? Thinking about practical things? Not to be torn apart by fear?

At two o'clock in the afternoon, the ticket collector ends his shift. Another worker takes his place and he says, "Watch out for this kid."

And this man helps me too.

He tells me to stay seated next to him. He pulls out a cirióla from his bag and gives me half of it along with the potato omelet.

CHAPTER SIX

It's raining cats and dogs. Perhaps it's the beginning of another global flood that will wipe everyone from the earth, good and bad. Maybe God has had enough of the evil people. Maybe he's decided to flood the world.

Is there a new Noah somewhere? Another Ark? Has he got the pairs of animals on it and all his family and now he's just waiting for the rain to destroy the world?

I don't want the destruction of the world. Not by God or by men. I don't want to end up in a thousand pieces because of a bomb. I don't want to be buried in rubble. I don't want to be robbed by the Germans. I don't want to drown in the water of the flood.

Is it so hard to live in peace?

The streets are full of puddles. They're like mirrors that reflect the buildings, the cloudy sky, the branches of trees that have lost almost all their leaves.

A woman gets on the tram. She's wearing men's clunky boots. She's so tired that when she sits down she closes her eyes.

She has small feet inside big shoes. She must have filled them with newspaper sheets or patches to be able to walk. But she walks badly. There's a blister stained with blood on her ankle.

After a while, having caught her breath, she tells the ticket collector about the lorry-loads of Jews that continue to drive around Rome.

"One told me they are new Germans. They arrived last night to do the dirty work. They don't know the roads and they make mistakes. Some lorries have even ended up in the countryside. Just imagine how those poor guys feel!"

"They told me," says another woman, "that the soldiers went to the Colosseum, Piazza del Popolo, Piazza San Pietro. They took photos to send home with lots of love!"

"As if," someone says. "In Piazza San Pietro they stopped to snub the pope. It was like they were telling him, 'See? We're under your windows. We do as we please.' "

"And the fascists?" asks the tired woman.

"Oh, those! They say they didn't know anything about the raid." We're all listening. "After the armistice the Germans don't trust them anymore. But that's a lie. The fascists knew all right. Even Mussolini knew it. But nobody lifted a finger to stop them."

I think back to the girl who said that we Jews don't have rights. That we are like things. That everyone can do whatever they want to us.

She's right and it's nice that a Catholic (had she been Jewish, she would not have challenged the fascist) speaks out in defense of us Jews. She put her life at risk to say we, too, have rights.

When I get off the tram, I'll go find her. I'll tell her I admire her so much and that I think she's a heroine like those of the cinema.

I'll ask Attilio to help me find her. He knows those here in Rome who are in the armed resistance, so he must know her too. Even if they don't expose themselves. Attilio once told me those people have to be invisible.

Attilio's name carries with it those of the others: Guido, David, Marco, Luigi, Moses.

The names come back to my mind along with the faces of my friends. Laughter as we splash the water from the fountain on each other, as we blow up the stick playing nizza e bastone, as we throw stones with the ammazzafionna.

While we play.

We play, yes, even though we work hard and bring home money. We're kids. We want to have fun.

Forget the war. Pretend life is good. The first ticket collector forgot to take his scarf back. Now that evening has fallen, the cold has increased. I spread the scarf over my shoulders and it warms me.

I doze off. When I wake, discouragement overcomes me. I miss my mom. An angry voice rises inside, telling me not to be a bird of ill omen. I have to think of her as free. Safe. I must want this with all my strength. The only way things come true is if you want them in that way.

With all my might, I want Ginotta Piazza to jump off the truck and fool those pimps that wanted her as a servant in their houses. Now she's waiting for me somewhere. Looking forward to getting back home. She'll be making the cacio e pepe there. Singing "Soli soli nella notte," then later sewing rags with the Singer machine that I'll resell to Campo de' Fiori.

I stay on the tram even when night falls. The driver goes to the depot but I have nowhere to go. This afternoon people said the Germans are still hunting the Jews.

The depot is dark.

When the driver turns off the engine, two people come up. One is the first ticket collector. He tells me his name is Mario. He holds a shank and a blanket.

In the shank is hot broth with a few pieces of potato and a beaten egg.

"Eat," he says.

The young man next to him (it must be his son, since they look like two peas in a pod) pulls something from his pocket. It's an apple. He hands it to me.

"It's washed," he says. "You can eat it with the whole peel."

I'm not used to certain delicacies like fruit. When I find something, I eat it as it is, without thinking whether it's washed or not. When I eat apricots I even eat the stone. I crush the rind and eat the pulp. It's only bitter sometimes because the rest is as sweet as an almond. Mom taught me to do this.

The other people leave the tram.

I stay on.

Before I eat, I put my hands around the shank to warm them.

No one's bringing hot broth and a blanket to Mom. I'm sure she's suffering.

The angry voice shouts at me. Ginotta is also safe. A kind soul has brought her something to eat.

"Don't be a bird of ill omen, Manue!" Mom says.

The broth is tasty. They even put cheese in it.

As I eat, I force myself to think of something nice. I don't want tragedy in my life. I've never accepted it. That's why I ran away when Grandma said Jews are a persecuted people.

I escape from the ghetto as soon as possible and go to the rich parts of the city. My eyes are filled with beauty. From an open window, a piano song comes out. The streets are clean and the gardens full of flowers. Here the war, if there is one, has not sown ugliness and destruction.

I try to fall asleep but can't. Everything's dark here. It's cold. But mostly my mind is full of thorny thoughts.

I'm shivering. I count sheep, but it doesn't work. In my mind I count the windows of Via della Reginella. Then those of Via di Sant'Ambrogio. Then those of Via Panicale. I remember them all and don't lose count, but sleep still doesn't come.

CHAPTER SEVEN

I am woken by the whine of a cat.

I open my eyes and don't understand. Reaching out, I feel for Nando in the bed. There's nothing but emptiness and, under my back, the tram seats. Then I remember everything.

The Germans. The trucks.

I have to run to save Mom!

Her scream bursts in my ears. "Resciùd." I hear the anger as she told Settimia I'd gotten myself into Jonàv's mouth.

"Manue," she seems to say. "Don't mess around. Woe to you if the Germans get you!"

Her voice is so real, so close that, for a moment I think I'm still in Via della Reginella. She's looking out the window checking where the gunshots are coming from.

But no more shooting.

No more war.

No more madmen who want to become the masters of the world and exterminate the dirty Jews who ruin their race.

No more pain.

No more fear.

"Enough! Enough!" I shout, beating my fist against the glass. I hit so hard it hurts, then I calm down a bit. The pain in my hand distracts me from the pain in my heart.

If Mom were here, she'd say, "Always making trouble, Manue!" but she'd say it without believing it.

She knows I don't make trouble. That I don't seek misfortune. That I don't look for it. I'm clever like her. I got strength and character from her. The shape of my mouth, even my smile. Everyone tells me when I smile I look like Mom.

The cat returns slowly. He knows that time is mortal for him too. In Rome, there isn't even one cat left. They have been killed by the best restaurants to serve them, as if they were rabbits, to the Germans and the fascist hierarchs, so people say.

But it's not true. The cats were eaten by all the hungry people who descended upon Rome after September 8. They thought they would be safe in the city of the pope.

"The Americans bombing the pope? No way," they said.

And instead. . . in San Lorenzo it was terrible.

"Manue, don't go there," Mom said.

But I was curious. I had heard the bangs, felt the earth shaking, the low planes dropping hundreds of bombs.

In the shelter, there were those who cried. Those who prayed. I held my little sister tight, telling her the bombing would be over soon, that it was like in the movies, where nothing happens for real. The blood is tomato and the bombs are like the firecrackers that the Catholics shoot off on New Year's Eve. She didn't believe it. She's a little girl, but not dumb, and she kept shaking, so I hugged her tightly.

The next day I asked Attilio if we could see where they had bombed. He immediately answered yes. Or rather, he said he was considering whether or not to ask me to accompany him.

"Why?" I asked.

"You might be shocked."

"I have a strong stomach," I said, boasting.

But as we got closer, I felt the sweat running down my back. It wet my forehead and slid from my temples to my neck.

The road was massacred. Everywhere holes, shards, glass, dust and stones, gutted buildings, beams protruding from open ceilings, scraps of curtains hanging from window stumps.

"Shall we go back?" he asked.

"No."

But later, when I saw a hand attached to an arm, missing everything else, and pieces of body scattered in the rubble, I felt sick. I leaned against a wall and threw up the almost-nothing I had in my stomach.

There were dead people on all sides.

An old woman called, "Remooo, Annina, Marcello! Answer, for God's sake!"

Women were crying, but even worse, there were women and children who had died. The bombs had struck shelters where the defenseless were seeking refuge.

An old man dug with his hands and shouted, "Damn Mussolini!" He was digging and shouting, "Damn, why aren't you down here?" No one told him to shut up.

If the fascists had heard him, they would have shot him in the forehead.

"Let's go," said Attilio.

We took the Verano Road, but it was worse. Part of the boundary wall had blown up along with the graves next to it. There were shattered graves, devastated trees, statues, and marble in pieces all the way to the street.

"Let's go," said Attilio, dragging me.

At one point I was no longer able to take a step.

I don't know how long we stayed there. The pope arrived to bless the dead lined up in front of the cemetery. The people kept quiet and prayed.

But it was when the king arrived in the limousine that the people got angry. They pelted the car with stones. Someone shouted, "We don't need your charity! We want peace, enough with this damn war!" Mostly women shouted and cried and threw stones against the king, who turned the car around and ran away.

Now in the darkness of this depot, the memories seem like scenes from a movie I don't want to see. Who knows if there is a medicine that erases the memories?

It's a bloody war, yes, with the Germans at home and the Americans who keep bombing. They throw balloons that look like toys from the planes. Instead they're phosphorous bombs. Little bottles full of stuff that hits the ground, explodes, and unleashes hell.

In the end, Attilio managed to get me out of there. He told me to look at the end of the street and not where we put our feet.

When I got home, Mom saw I was upset. She didn't say anything. She knew that I'd gone to San Lorenzo and had been among the dead. She put a piece of soap in my hands and said, "Go down to the fountain. Wash yourself well."

I obeyed.

I went to the nearest fountain, took off my shirt, and soaped my body and face. I washed and rubbed and rinsed. Went back to soaping to get rid of the dust and the smell of death, but also to erase from my mind what I had seen.

With the memories, I failed. They are all here, as precise as a recent movie that the mind keeps rewatching.

CHAPTER EIGHT

The cat stopped meowing.
　Maybe he ran away. Maybe someone caught him. Grabbed him by the neck and put him into the pot.
　I open the window because the air in here has become heavy.
　From outside comes the smell of wet earth, of grass, of the wood burning in stoves.
　I think of the focaròla that Mom lights in the kitchen to keep us warm.
　There was this really cold winter and we burned, piece by piece, a large trunk.
　In the evening, lots of us gather around the focaròla. There's always someone, like old Lia, who tells stories. Some people's stomachs growl when they're hungry, but no one notices it.
　One story is of Rut, a widow who after ten years of loneliness found a new husband. Her mother-in-law helped her.

That name, Rut, makes me think of Rut, Tobia's daughter. She's twelve years old like me and sometimes she smiles at me.

What do I like about her?

Actually, I like everything. The way she talks, the way she walks, how she looks after her brothers. How she looks at me.

Why am I only noticing this now?

Perhaps before, I had only Ester on my mind and wasn't paying attention to others.

God, tell me they didn't take her. Tell me she is somewhere safe!

I try to remember when I last saw her. She was in the Piazza delle Tartarughe, standing near the fountain. And the time before that? And the time before that?

Sleep comes but I don't notice.

The driver finds me curled up under the blanket.

"Hey, little kid," he says, touching my arm.

I wince, open my eyes wide. Where am I?

They've turned on the lights in the depot. Through the open doors I can hear the voices of those who work with the trams.

In a moment I'm on my feet. I fold the blanket, put it on the seat, and sit on it.

The driver is a skinny man, with the neck of a cockerel in his oversized shirt. "Are you cold?" he asks.

I shake my head.

"Were you able to sleep?"

I lower my head. I can tell he wants to ask me something. Maybe how I escaped the Germans, how I managed to save myself, but he thinks better of it. He hands me a bag.

"Eat," he tells me.

Inside is a whole ciriòla with a few pieces of cheese. He also hands me a bottle.

"It's small, but you can fill it at the fountain." He rubs his hands hard to keep them warm, occasionally coughing.

The ticket collector asks him how his wife is.

"Always the same," he says. After another coughing fit he says, "Time to go."

I split the ciriόla into three parts, one for breakfast, one for lunch, and one for dinner. When have I ever had a whole ciriόla just to myself?

It's dark outside. It's five o'clock and Rome seems empty, but I know it's not. On the streets there are already ambulances. There are rag-and-bone men. There are those who search among the rubbish for something to eat. Those who line up for cigarettes. For every pack of cigarettes, they will give you a kilo of bread, but you must have ration cards. Not all Jews have them.

We took turns lining up for cigarettes. We also

got into lines for coal. The coalman is on Via dei Falegnami. Some people start standing in line from Piazza Campitelli at eight in the evening.

When it's my turn, I line up at 2:00 a.m. and stand there until six in the morning. Four hours in line that covers no more than four hundred meters.

All for what?

For a bag of coal that gets scarcer every day.

At first no one gets on the tram. It's Sunday and for Catholics it's a feast day.

Our festive Saturday has turned into a day of tragedy.

Who could have said that on Friday, when we were sitting in the cinema watching Gino Bechi living out his love affair with the girl on the train?

That afternoon Mom wasn't quiet, come to think of it.

In the movie, the police stopped the two strangers. They didn't have their papers and the police took them to jail. Mom immediately opened her purse to check if our documents were still there. She was nervous. She turned everything over until she found them.

"Without these, you are lost," she said.

Even with these, you are lost, I thought, because it says you are a Jew. You are worthless. But I did not want to make her sad.

She went back to watching the movie. Her face lost its fear and became happy again, especially when the man and girl were released from prison.

Throughout that story (but also afterward, until the Germans arrived in our neighborhood) she seemed as happy as she did a long time ago, when we were not called dirty Jews. When we were not considered citizens without rights.

The bells of the Borgo are calling people to Mass. I like the sound of bells.

Mom does too. She says they make beautiful music. She says that when she sits at the Singer sewing machine doing the small repairs that she trades for a little bit of beans or vegetables or flour or whatever.

She's someone who invents every little trick to fill our plates. She always says that we are lucky because we have a roof over our heads. She says this when she sees people huddled in the street, fighting over a piece of pavement sheltered by a balcony.

"We have a home. Don't complain. Think of those who are worse off."

I think about it, yes. Especially at night when it's freezing. Then, the sheets seem wet and we go to bed wearing our clothes and coats.

When it's really cold and you don't have coal and no wood to burn and it's raining outside, life looks really bad. Then you think of those lying on the ground, without cardboard for shelter, and you swallow your complaints and thank God.

It's daylight and the tram is now full. Every now and then the ticket collector looks at me. I think the one from yesterday, Mario, is some kind of boss who gave his colleagues the order to protect me.

What a responsibility! If the Germans find out they're protecting a Jew, they'll take them to Germany, and goodbye, family.

These people on the tram are all angels that God has sent me.

I do everything not to stand out. I sit there quietly, with the paper bag containing the ciriolà under my shirt and the scarf covering the lump.

At Piazza dell' Indipendenza, a man elbows his way up. He is dressed as a gentleman and behaves like a boor. He keeps talking to the woman accompanying him.

"In the ghetto alone, they took about a thousand. Then others around Rome. A nice cleanup."

She looks uncomfortable. He seems to notice and purposely speaks louder. He says that the operation was conducted impeccably. That the shots outside the ghetto were served to keep us indoors. That the Germans have acted on the Sabbath because it is the Jewish day of rest.

"Understand?" he says. "They rest and we work!"

He doesn't need to wear a black shirt to understand that he's a fascist.

The other passengers turn away from him.

Only one agrees with him. "The Germans are iron men. They have a clear final purpose. They don't back down like some Italian slackers!"

The reference to the king fleeing to Apulia with Badoglio. Even I understand although I know nothing about politics.

"Therefore," the second man says, "they are the nation that will rule the world." He adjusts the glasses on his nose. He says the Jews from the roundup were taken to the Military College in Via della Lungara to be strip-searched.

The other bursts out laughing. He has two gold teeth in his mouth.

I stare at him angrily. I want to remember this one. I want to remember him when the war is over. I want to tie him to a chair and throw a lot of fleas on him. I hope they will eat him. Get into his mouth and his eyes. Devour his heart.

I close my eyes and grit my teeth. The rage is so strong that I would smash his face with my fist.

The ticket collector grazes my arm.

When I open my eyes, I realize that the fascist is looking at me, puzzled. "What are you always doing here?' he asks me. "I saw you yesterday too. Don't you have a home?"

"He's my nephew!" the ticket collector says. Then, slamming the clamp on one of the iron handles he says, "Go ahead. Come on. There's no room back here!"

The fascist keeps looking at me. He doesn't seem convinced. I breathe slowly, without taking my eyes off his. I don't want to look scared, and I don't want him to think of me as being trapped.

"Don't you want to move?" asks the ticket collector. "Go on! Go ahead!'

At last, the two fascists who were making all the noise get out of the way.

They took them to the Military College to strip-search them.

What does that mean?

The one with the gold teeth turns to look at me again. Like he wants to remember my face, too, and certainly not to throw a lot of fleas at me. He's dressed as a gentleman, but he's a boor.

It doesn't take a lot of intelligence to understand where he gets his money. If he reports me to the Germans, he earns one thousand lire because I'm a child. He gets paid five thousand lire for a man and three thousand for a woman. Those are the prices the Germans have put on us.

There are people who got rich this way. By

putting Jews in the hands of the Germans. Entire families were betrayed, for money, by people they believed were their friends. We know some of these people. We learned that they played dirty and now we shun them.

There are others we don't even suspect. Only at the end of the war will they be discovered. They will deny it. They'll swear they never ratted anyone out. They'll say they have a clear conscience, and will call God as a witness.

Even Celeste, the girl from Via della Reginella, who is so beautiful they nicknamed her "The Star of the Port," is a snitch. Later, when they tell me this, I won't believe it.

Since the fascist keeps his eyes on me, the ticket collector opens his bag, gives me a piece of his loaf of bread, and says, "Eat! Otherwise your mother will yell at me."

This gesture would convince anyone. In times of black hunger, you don't share bread with one who is not of the same blood as you.

I know where the Military College on Via della Lungara is. Inside, there's a large courtyard. Sometimes I pass around there. It's full of soldiers doing exercises.

The words of the man in glasses keep running through my mind, especially "stripping them."

Have the Jews been taken into that courtyard where they are searched for any money or jewelry they may be hiding?

Definitely.

The fifty kilos of gold wasn't enough for them. They think we possess who-knows-how-much wealth and they're putting their hands on us to get it.

To understand, I try to pay attention to the other passengers' conversations, but no one talks about the Via Lungara. And I, who would like to ask a hundred questions, must keep quiet so as not to arouse anyone's suspicions.

It's drizzling.

The streetlights are on as if it was afternoon. The bells continue to call people to Mass, and they are flocking to church.

I think of the girl who asked the fascist if he really knew the meaning of "You shall love your neighbor as yourself." I see her as she rebels against the one who wanted to shut her mouth up.

". . . to via della Lungara, yes," someone says. He adds that during the night relatives and friends of the prisoners went to ask for news, to bring comfort items. But the Germans crammed everyone into rooms where the windows were nailed shut, fearing someone would escape, and according to the documents, they are now dividing the Jews from the non-Jews, from mixed blood.

That's what it means that they are stripping them. They're looking at papers, checking the documents.

What's Mom going to do?

Mom isn't at the Military College, the angry voice screams in my mind. *She isn't there!"*

"But where they are taking them after?" someone asks.

"To Germany," another says.

It's not possible!

CHAPTER NINE

We are around Piazza Venezia. I remember it vividly. It was full to the bursting point. People going crazy for the duce every time he appeared on the balcony. Flags. Hats in the air. Applause. Children carried on their parent's shoulders so's not to miss anything.

He stood there, chest out, hands in his belt, chin forward.

When he spoke, the square became silent. As soon as he closed his mouth, a frenzy of applause and shouts erupted.

At first, I was affected by the whole thing. The square going crazy. Him on the balcony talking to the Italians. He was also speaking to me. I'm Italian like the others, so I, like the others, dressed up as a balilla to go to school.

But, even then, I didn't like his speeches because I don't like war. It brings hunger, starvation, and the death of so much innocent flesh, as my grandmother said remembering the First World War.

When he turned against the Jews, I no longer went to hear him.

His speeches made me angry. I saw that, to him, only those like him were worthwhile: pure Aryan, fighting, and evil. And we Jews are none of this.

On June 10, 1940, when he made the declaration of war on the British and French, Attilio dragged me under the balcony. He said, "This speech will lead Italy to ruin."

I was nine years old. What could I understand?

The square exploded in a roar of joy, as if someone had announced the arrival of the Messiah. Attilio took me by the hand and dragged me to the ghetto. As we walked, he mimicked the duce's words.

"The hour of irrevocable decisions. . .The plutocratic and reactionary democracies of the West. . ."

"What does that mean?" I asked.

"I'll explain to you later." But then he met some friends from Quadraro and followed them.

I remember everything about that day.

Mussolini saying that the declaration of war had already been delivered to the ambassadors of Great Britain and France. That we could no longer submit to blackmail. And everybody clapping their hands. Everyone saying "Bravooo!" Whistling, waving flags, and shouting.

Now there is silence.

Mussolini is in the north. The king is in Apulia. The Americans are bombing. The Germans are in charge. The fascists (to save their skins and keep the invaders at bay) denounce us Jews, who must pay for everyone because we are double traitors.

And maybe Mom is in Via della Lungara worrying about my brother who's sick. Maybe she's wondering if we took him to the hospital. If we give him medicines.

Or wondering if I made it out.

Or maybe she doesn't have time to think about anything because the Germans are searching her to see if she still has gold on her.

The rest of the day passes in the same way as yesterday. The tram goes round, then stops, starts up again, people get on, some chatter, some others don't have the breath to say a word, some others still don't want to open their mouths.

I get off twice to go to the bathroom, to relieve myself. Then I returned to my seat, next to the ticket collector, the blanket folded on the seat, the blue scarf around my neck.

Looking at myself in the reflection of the glass, I think that if the one with the gold teeth wants to sell me to the Germans, all he has to say is, "It's the kid in the blue scarf, who's been on the circular." And they take me. So as a precaution, I take off my scarf, put it in the middle of the blanket, and sit on it.

"Badoglio has declared war on Germany," shouts a boy with a newspaper in his hand.

"Old news," says the ticket collector.

I don't remember this.

"Fake news," says a guy with his cap pulled down almost to his eyes. "Mussolini has not yet been defeated."

"But he has made the Republic of Salò."

"It is a puppet government, wanted and maneuvered by Hitler. Mussolini no longer counts for anything. Really. Nothing!"

"Yes, but the Allies are in Salerno. How do you think it ends?"

No one answers.

Badly! I think.

We'll end up in civil war, as Uncle Cesare said the day he showed up home with a chicken, bartered for two packs of cigarettes.

The tram empties and I pull out the last piece of ciriòla and eat. The ticket collector also eats. The driver, on the other hand, sticks to his bottle.

When we are stopped at a traffic light, near Santa Maria Maggiore, I see the windows of a building lit up. The ceilings are full of painted figures, the chandeliers sparkle, all around are statues.

I feel I'm in a movie. Men in uniform and elegantly dressed women raise glasses and toast. It seems that the war does not exist for them. They laugh, their mouths open, their glasses in the air, cigarettes between their fingers.

I keep watching as the tram pulls away. After a bend, the building disappears.

The glitter of the lighted chandeliers stays in my eyes. In Via della Reginella we have cheap light, one bulb per room, and if you light one, the others don't turn on.

Wealth puts you in beauty, I think. Money allows you luxury. Heated buildings. The glassware and jewelry. The paintings on all the walls. Someone to serve you at the table. To clean your house. Your belly is always full.

The poor endure cold, ugliness, and hunger.

Evening falls.

The tram is empty. People lock themselves in their homes. Those who are homeless hole up under bridges or in front of churches or in the basement of some building with its front door left open.

I look out the window. I just see black. Not a single star.

The word *star* reminds me of the Catholics' Christmas.

I'm friends with the Catholics. It's not true that they hate us all because we put Jesus Christ on the cross and so we are condemned to eternal disgrace. Not everyone thinks that way.

Besides, when you are on the street, they don't even know you're Jewish. You don't have it written on your forehead. They don't ask for your ID when you sell your rubber bands or wallets or rags. Here in Italy, fortunately, they don't force you to wear the yellow star on your arm.

At Christmas, I go to Largo di Torre Argentina. I stand by the theater, open an umbrella, and spread out the postcards with the nativity scene. There are the angels, the comet star, the mountains full of snow.

"Five postcards, one lira!" I shout. "Buy your postcards!"

And those coming out of the theater buy. Sometimes I even collect twenty lire, which is a lot.

Afterward, I return home feeling content either because I've earned some money or because I've enjoyed spending a few hours with wonderful company.

The ghetto fills me with immense sadness, prompting me to leave as soon as possible. It pains me to witness the misery, the hunger, and the fact that we as Jews must live as beggars. We are unable to obtain honorable professions.

Those who were once professors, doctors, engineers, or company executives now have to scrape by as best they can. They have jobs like ragpickers and peddlers.

At the depot I see Mario. He's brought the bowl, staying just long enough to ask how I am doing.

How am I doing? I think of Mom and long to be with her. But I don't say it. I shrug and that is already an answer.

"Come on, eat," he tells me.

I lower my head.

"Cover yourself well. Don't catch cold."

Tonight, he came alone. He didn't bring his son.

The bowl is hot. Inside there is spaghetti cacio e pepe.

I eat spaghetti and tears, thinking of Mom.

I eat spaghetti and tears and almost don't notice.

CHAPTER TEN

It's daylight again and the tram is full.

A man holding a briefcase and wearing professor's glasses says they've taken the Jews from Via della Lungara to the Tiburtina station. They're loading them onto a long train. They're heading for Germany.

Mom is not on that train, I'm sure of that.

In a few days I'll see her. And we'll go back to the nice life we had before, because the most important thing is to be all together. The rest doesn't matter.

How I miss her. I even miss her silences, which used to make me melancholy because I'm a talker and she is measured in speech.

Someone says the Germans are still hunting the Jews. That those they've caught are still too few. He says that Hitler is angry with the Italians who declared war on Germany and they have to send thousands of Jews to appease his anger.

May he end up in Jonav's mouth!

The tram is packed now. People bumping into each other, elbowing each other to get ahead. It's normal. Today is Monday. Those who have work hurry to get there.

I put my head to the glass and look out.

Today is October 18. At Tiburtina station there's a train full of Jews. No one is allowed to go near it. No one is allowed to see it.

What a dreadful time!

I'd like to skip two or three years and find myself in a future where there is peace. Where nobody calls you a dirty Jew. Betta will have married in the meantime, and Mom is holding one of Betta's children.

Amid the chaos I hear a voice say, "Manue! Is that really you?"

I turn around and see Davide, who lives in Via della Reginella. He looks at me as if I were a ghost.

"What are you doing here?" he asks, murmuring. "Your father thinks you're dead. He thinks the Germans have taken you and your mother."

"The Germans didn't take him?"

"No."

"My brothers?"

"No."

It feels like the weight in my heart is getting lighter.

"Where are they?"

"In Borgo. At your aunt's place. Come on!" He takes me by the arm and drags me toward the door.

I turn to the ticket collector, who smiles at me happily. He must have suffered for me, both he and all the others who have helped me. They must have thought I was alone in the world, that I had no family.

Instead, I do have a family and that is an important thing.

"Thank you," I tell him. "Thank you all."

"Take care," he says.

David pushes me toward the exit and I find myself in the street.

The blanket and scarf are left on the seat, folded, the scarf inside the blanket.

I forgot to tell the ticket collector that he must return them to Mario, but Davide couldn't wait to get off, to send me to Dad.

I would find out later about the one with the gold teeth. I guessed right. He really was a spy who denounced me to the SS.

Davide's sister stayed on the tram that morning because she had to get off at Flaminio. She said that at the next stop two Germans and a fascist got on. They went straight to the ticket collector and asked him about the little boy.

"Little boy?" the ticket collector said, like someone falling off the turnip truck. "This place is full of kids who get on and off and they drive me crazy. Don't talk to me about kids or I'll become a hyena!"

The fascist told him not to be clever. "The boy with the blue scarf," he said, specifying. "The one who sat here all the time." He pointed to the place that for almost three days was mine. At that moment the seat was occupied by a nun.

"Was there a little boy sitting here?" the fascist asked.

"If you say so, it will be true. I, however, do not remember it. With all the people passing by, I can't remember a green scarf."

"Blue!"

"Green. Blue. What difference does it make? Every kid is God's punishment. If you catch him, give him a slap as well from me."

The Germans started screaming. The fascist said he was sure of what he had seen.

"What have you seen?" asked one of them.

"A dirty Jew."

Then an old woman approached him. She said he was right. She had seen me. Yes, I had just got off the tram. "These Jews are like weeds!" she said in a nasty tone. "How do you get rid of them once and for all?"

"What do you think we are doing?" he answered, satisfied. "Did you see which way he went?"

The ticket collector turned pale.

"Of course, I saw him! He went toward Trastevere. Run, you will find him!"

They got out in a hurry and ran toward Trastevere.

The ticket collector started to breathe again and a small smile appeared on his mouth. The old woman gave him a wink. She had sent them the opposite way that I was going.

CHAPTER ELEVEN

We arrived at Aunt Sara's house around ten o'clock. She married Giorgio Proietti, who is from a Catholic family, so they live in Borgo, in the Vatican. When Dad sees me, he doesn't believe it's me in the flesh and blood. He reaches out to touch me, brushes my hair and my cheeks.

"Is that you, really?" he asks. Then he hugs me so hard it hurts. When he lets me go, I realize his eyes are like tomatoes. He's been crying for two days. He asks how I managed to save myself. I tell him everything, really everything, from when the shooting started, to when Mom went down to go to Termini and warn him not to come back to the ghetto.

"It's all my fault," he says with a murmur. "I told her to go home, take you kids and run to Testaccio, where I would have joined you. If I had held her back, she wouldn't be in that truck now."

"No," I said. "She would have gone back to the ghetto. She wouldn't have tried to save herself knowing we were in danger. She would never have done that."

I'm not telling a lie to get a little pain off his chest. It really would have been like that. I know Mom too well. She would have quarreled if he had tried to hold her back. We children are the most important thing in life for her.

Dad stares at me.

His eyes, which before were full of pain, become doubtful, then show a kind of relief. It's not his fault that Ginotta went back to the ghetto. She would have gone back anyway.

He blows his nose. "Tell me everything from the beginning. What time was it when the German took her?"

"About half past five."

"Who was with her in the truck?"

"Settimia with her mother and sisters. Moses, too, now that I think of it."

"How did she throw you out of the truck?"

"I don't know. I was just standing there, stunned. I wanted to save her, but I didn't know how. She was angry. She said that I'd got myself into Jonàv's mouth. I didn't understand, and at that moment, I don't know how, she threw me out and I found myself on the street."

"And then? What happened then?"

I tell him about Via di Sant'Ambrogio. About the German distracted by the cow. About Anna's house. About the second truck at the Portico d'Ottavia.

I talk to him and it seems I'm living everything again, like in a movie. It's so vivid, my heart starts beating fast, like when you run so fast not to get caught.

Aunt Sara stops me. Tells me to calm down. To drink a little water.

I obey because I'm out of breath, and it's difficult for me to speak.

In my mind, I go back to Monte Savello and see myself walking. Eyes down, hands in my pockets, rain in my hair, down my back, inside my shoes.

"And then?" Dad asks.

I take a breath. Another sip of water. "Then I got on the tram. And I stayed there until this morning when Davide told me that you were here in Borgo."

"You were always on the tram? Even at night?"

"Yes, at the depot. They even fed me."

"Why didn't you come to Auntie's?"

"I knew the Germans were looking for us all over Rome. It seemed to me that on the tram, among so many people, I could hide better."

Dad lowers his head, then says, "Tell me about your mother again. Don't forget anything. All the details. From the beginning."

I start again.

Betta, who had gone with her aunt to a neighbor's, comes in the house. When she sees me, she throws herself at my neck and wants to hear the whole story from the beginning.

"And you?" I finally ask. "How did you save yourselves? Where did you hide?"

We're in the bedroom, among the relatives. Only Mom is missing. Of our whole family, they took only her.

"After you went out," Betta says, "we waited. But you didn't come back. I looked out and saw the Germans weren't just taking only the men, like Mom said. But also the women and children. I told everyone we had to escape immediately.

"Down at the gate, I met Aunt Rebecca. She told me not to go to the square but to escape by the other road. We hid in her house. She wanted to come here to Borgo and I told myself it was better if we went back.

"I took Via della Reginella. Then I heard Mom's voice screaming like a madman. 'Betta, resciùd! Resciùd.' I went to open the door but she said, 'No, no! That way!'

"We went back to the side of the synagogue. I turned and saw a German grab her and slam her head against the wall."

I remain breathless.

We all remain breathless.

For a while there's only the sound of a large alarm clock on the drawer chest. It echoes in my ears as if a hammer is beating time on a bell. I look at my father, who has started crying again. Betta is crying too.

Aunt Sara takes the little brothers to another room. Nando follows her.

The air seems thick, so hard that I struggle to breathe. I have the feeling of being underwater again, like when the German put the machine gun on my chest.

Then, to break the kind of spell into which we have all fallen, I ask, "Are you sure Mom is in Tiburtina?"

Betta looks at Dad, then at me. "Yes," she says. "Nobody can get near her. The Germans killed three people who were trying to escape. They shoot anyone who comes close."

Tears keep running down Dad's face. There's almost nothing left of the stern man, who used to frighten us with one look. Knowing that Mom is in the hands of the Germans is a tragedy for him.

I, however, don't want to give up.

Mom wouldn't want to. She'd say we must react, look for a solution instead of crying.

"Even if they take her to Germany," I say, "it doesn't mean she won't come back. She'll come back, it's certain. They take her to serve in a rich person's house. You know what? She'll be better than us! Sure, separation is bad, but it doesn't last forever!"

I say this loudly to convince everyone, especially myself.

But I'm not just saying it. I really believe it. As soon as the war ends, she'll come back home, all smiling and beautiful, ready to scold us if the room is messy or we argue. We just must be patient.

"As soon as the war ends, Mom will come back. How much shall we bet?" I ask.

Betta says yes.

Dad throws his head back, stares at the roof as if he wants to read the future.

My sister and I look at each other. We understand that, from now on, until he gets better, the two of us must take care of the family.

When it's lunchtime, Auntie calls us. She has managed to get some potatoes, cheese, and hard bread, so she's making meatballs. It looks like a feast day. But it's not. There are twelve of us at the table and no one is talking.

All you can hear is the sound of forks tapping on the plates. The silence is too hard to bear. Dad is not eating. Slumped in his chair, he looks straight ahead and seems to forget about the rest of the world.

Uncle, then, tells what happened the two days

I was on the tram. But it's like my ears were full of wax. He speaks. Aunt adds something but I don't even hear them. They look like fish inside a fishbowl, opening and closing their mouths for no reason.

My mind is in Tiburtina. I know the station well. I sell souvenirs to the soldiers there. In a while I'll go there.

I can't believe that the Germans are shooting at those who come near.

Besides, I know a secret entrance that leads directly to the tracks, without going through the main entrance.

I don't trust what others say. I want to see it with my own eyes—the train leaving for Germany. I'll hurry up and eat and go.

I am deep in these thoughts when someone knocks at the door.

The blood freezes in our veins. Uncle signals us to silence. He approaches the door. "Who is it?" he asks.

"Claudio," they answer from outside.

Claudio is his brother, also a Catholic. In this house, we Jews should consider ourselves safe. The Germans don't come to break down the doors of the houses in the Vatican.

He gives us the news we don't want to hear. The train full of Jews, with the sealed wagons, has left for Germany.

CHAPTER TWELVE

We stay in Borgo at my aunt's house for three days. Then we go back to Via della Reginella.

What are we doing here? The Germans haven't come back to the ghetto. One person told me that right now in Rome there's no place safer. Our house, without Mom, is like a body without a soul. We miss her voice, the noise of the Singer, her standing at the window waiting for dad, the smell of the food she used to prepare. It is true that we are not alone, uncles and cousins live in the other rooms, but it is also true that every family huddles around its parents and, in ours, we don't have Mom anymore. Dad is as if he were not there. Since Mom is away, he spends his days crying, unable to do anything. It's like he has lost the reason to live. He no longer has that energy that made him get up at three in the morning, wash and dress himself, go out, come back to eat, and go out again, go and buy souvenirs to sell to the Germans. Sitting on the bed, staring at nothing, he looks like the seventh brother that Betta has to look after. Who would have thought that he would end up like this? We have always been afraid of him. He is strict, rigorous, an iron man, able to get the better of even those who are twice as big.

A new life begins for us.

At first glance it appears to be the same as always. Betta takes Mom's place. I realize that if I don't start working, we'll starve. So I pick up the sack, put it on my shoulder, and go house to house asking people if they have rags to sell me.

Rome is full of angry Germans and confused Italians. After September 8, Badoglio, from Apulia, declared Rome an "open city." This means the Allies could enter without fighting.

Attilio explained that this happens when there are cities full of history, of beauty, and art. He said it would be a sacrilege (that's exactly what he said, "sacrilege") to destroy it with bombs and cannon fire.

The Americans, however, didn't accept this because the Germans, on armistice day, swooped down on Rome and occupied it.

So much for preserving historical beauties and monuments. Rome became a battlefield.

The Americans bombing from the air. The Germans firing from the ground, doing raids, and arresting you for no reason. There are also those of the Resistance, especially those from the Quadraro. They sabotage, plant bombs, and try to make life difficult for the occupier.

I found Attilio here in the ghetto after a week.

When I saw him I couldn't believe it. I hugged him tightly, and for the first time since the morning Mom was taken away, I felt happy. I asked if everyone in his family had survived. He answered yes. On the morning of the sixteenth, when his mother went to the terrace to hang out the laundry, she saw the SS coming. She ran to wake her husband and children and they fled over the rooftops, finding refuge in a convent.

"We didn't stay there long. Convent life is not suitable for us," Attilio said.

I walk through the streets with a sack over my shoulder calling, "Women. The ragman has arrived. Money and rags, women." And when the windows open and someone calls me, I give a big smile.

It's the smile that makes me work so hard. I realize this because it's how it works for me. If I see someone who is sad, I run away. Everyone has their own tragedy. I can't take the crying anymore. So people go looking for a cheerful face, a smile that conveys sympathy, a will to live.

The women call me and I climb the steps two

by two. I buy what they offer me, and sometimes, if I see that someone is too lonely, I tell them some story. Like the one about the priest and the umbrella that is becoming my warhorse.

Business is good and after a few weeks, I manage to rent a cart and improve my trade. No more sacks on my back. I buy and sell shards (plates, glasses, jugs, and ornaments) that I pick up in a little shop near the Portico d'Ottavia. I display the merchandise prominently on the cart and head for the rich streets.

"Shards," I shout now. "Shards and money." And also, "Rags," because the rags are easier to peddle. Especially when the stuff belongs to the dead and so the family gets rid of the clothing of those who have suffered too much.

"Rags and shreds! Womeeeen!"

The Germans don't come back to the ghetto. It's November and their lives in half-free Italy become more and more difficult. The people are tired of everything. Of the Germans and the fascists, but also of the Americans and the British who keep dropping bombs and killing hundreds of civilians. So far from the open city!

"If they hurry up and come!" they say of the Allies.

Of course, some fanatics of Mussolini call both the king and Badoglio traitors. They pray that the

Germans will hurry up and win and eliminate all those who changed flags on September 8. But they are few in number. It would be better for them to leave if they don't want to end up being skinned alive by those who can't take it anymore.

We heard that in Naples, from September 27 to 30, all hell broke loose. It all started with a sailor killed at the Vomero. The Neapolitans became furious. After years of harassment, abuse, killings, imprisonment, torture, and violence, they said "Enough!"

They staged a rebellion against the Germans in every street, in every alley, emerging from underground, even from the graves, to drive them out. The women fought with more anger than the men. Someone told me that one woman knocked out a tank by throwing a marble slab from a chest of drawers from the balcony.

In short, on the morning of October 1, when the Americans entered the city, they didn't have to fire a single bullet. The people had already done everything.

Maybe it wasn't exactly like that, but that's the essence of the speech. I admire so much the Neapolitans. They organized the poor's rebellion. They didn't use tanks or bombs from the sky. It was a rebellion with an improvised weapon first, then with weapons stolen from the Germans.

This kind of popular fury still doesn't exist here in Rome. Those in the Resistance are few, mostly communists. Attilio is a friend to some of them, so I hear things.

The partisans hide out at the Quadraro. They organize sabotage and attacks on the Germans. But their numbers are too few. They can't move the whole population.

You know, here are the hierarchs. They're connected to Mussolini, who made the Republic of Salò. They can't wait to get back to Rome.

There's the pope, who keeps telling Catholics to do God's will, and nobody understands what that means anymore.

I know all these things because Attilio tells me and because, since I've been on the tram, I've learned to keep my ears wide open.

Before, I lived like a child, without taking an interest in politics. I have now realized that politics are in life and, if I understand it, I understand life. I understand there are duties, but also rights. Right and wrong laws. The oppressors and the oppressed.

So, even though I haven't completed all my schooling, I'm still learning.

And who is my teacher?

The street, because I learn all these things by passing under windows and shouting, "Shards and rags." By stopping at the drinking fountain. By standing with my cart in the shade, waiting for some woman to come and buy an ornament, a couple of plates, or glasses.

One morning, near Via Cavour, someone missing an arm says the Germans stopped trucks in Piazza San Pietro to show the pope they were in charge.

It was October 16.

"In heaven, on earth, and everywhere!" he said. "They believe themselves to be God and they decide who should live and who should die." He was so angry his face turned all red, the veins in his neck swelled. It seemed that his heart was going to burst at any moment.

People told him to calm down, things were done, there was no point in talking like that anymore.

"We should have intervened," he shouted, making himself, if it was possible, even redder. "We should not be accomplices!"

I stood with my little cart in the shelter of a doorway.

It had started to rain, and rags and shards were getting wet. I wanted to approach the man, tell him to be careful, that spies are everywhere. Tell him that if the Germans heard him, they would have taken him to the prison on Via Tasso, where political prisoners are tortured to death. But who was I to tell him to be careful? Just a street urchin and a kid.

Thank goodness his friend shuts him up. He links arms with him. Hurries him into a crossroad to who knows where.

"The Germans are God's punishment," says an old lady who witnessed the scene.

God's punishment. But could God be so bad as to have sent us those devils?

I no longer accept the idea of God sending you afflictions to punish you. Or to test your fidelity. Job had everything taken away from him before having it restored a hundredfold.

To me what I earn is enough. If I ask God for a favor, it's to bring Mom back home safe and sound. I'll take care of the rest.

Now the old lady approaches the cart. She looks at the broken pieces. Picks up an odd glass, and without asking me how much it was, she gives me five lire.

"That's too much," I tell her.

She seems poor and I don't want to take advantage of her. (With the Germans it's different. I never tell them that they have given me too much).

"I'm alone," she said. "What do I do with money?"

She gives me a smile, which is meant to be happy but is full of all the sadness in the world. Then she turns her back on me and walks, little by little, toward a palace. One of those noble ones, with large gates, and the doors that look like gold.

I go back to Via della Reginella. It doesn't have big gates with golden doors but is so full of noise, of people, kids screaming, that you never feel alone.

CHAPTER THIRTEEN

Betta prepares spaghetti with tomato sauce and a salad.

If I took Dad's place, she's become the mother of the family.

Some days I see her waiting for me at the window to see if I've brought the money for lunch. I tell her yes from a distance. She comes down, takes the money, and goes to buy what's needed.

We're at the table eating spaghetti when Bruno, Aunt Rosetta's son, rushes in. He says his father is with two fascists.

Immediately all us kids run to our room (which is the last one in the house, the one farthest down) and hide under the bed.

After a while the fascists come in. They approach the bed.

"Come on, come out from under there," they say.

We crawl out but as soon as they turn away, I

crawl back under the bed.

"Come on," they say to everyone. They must have guns, as no one tries to fight.

Before leaving, Betta throws two gold necklaces under the bed, meaning, "If you are in trouble, pawn these, and eat."

I don't breathe.

Footsteps of everyone gather in the kitchen.

Uncle Cesare says to leave the kids at home. "They're innocent. What harm have they done to you?"

"No whining!" says the meaner of the two fascists.

They go out onto the landing, leaving the door open. I can hear the heels beating on the steps with an increasingly lighter sound. I hear them on Via della Reginella.

"Cesare, where are you taking the kids?" says the produce vendor, but he immediately shuts up. He must have seen the fascists.

A deadly silence follows.

I stay under the bed for hours. I don't know how many. Four? Five? Who knows?

I come out when it's almost dark. Then I walk around each room. Look under the other beds and inside the cupboards to see if any of my cousins are hiding there. None.

There's only me.

I feel a deep sense of black despair. This house is

always full of people and chaos. Now there's a total emptiness. I walk around the rooms like a ghost. Twenty of us used to live here, and now I'm alone.

In the kitchen, on the table, there are still the plates with pasta that no one had time to finish. The jugs with water. The pieces of bread. A tomato stain stands out red in the middle of the tablecloth. It looks like blood to me. It seems to say, *You see? All gone. All killed. Your relatives.*

What do I do now?

I can't go out into the street. I don't know if there are other fascists around. I don't even look out the window.

I played here, in this home, with my cousins. There was the time I hid on the tettarello and stayed there for two hours, happy to have found the perfect hiding place. When they couldn't find me, and I got bored, I went down and learned that, rather than looking for me, they'd gone to the cinema without telling me!

The cinema makes me think of Gino Bechi, of that song of his which now seems to me like a disgrace. "Soli soli. . ."

I don't want to be alone! It would have been better to go with them.

The sadness is too much.

I open the wardrobe and stick my face into Mom's

good dress. The one she uses for weddings and parties. It's dark blue, like the sky before evening. I find her smell in it. And other smells, like apples. Her voice. The shape of her body.

I put my arms in the sleeves and hug myself and it's like Mom's hugging me. She's saying, "Manue. Be strong. You must go on. You can't stop. You can't give up."

Go on?

Where?

Without a family, life is a tragedy. Even happy days are a tragedy. Even days spent selling Christmas cards, or at the cinema, or at the hospital that seemed like the Grand Hotel.

But what a Grand Hotel!

I had twenty stitches from elbow to armpit, and the pain was powerful. I stayed warm. So what? I had a clean bed. So what? Life is ugly! Ugly and miserable, ugly and hopeless!

I cry and embrace myself with my arms like it's Mom.

I'm still here, despairing about my bitter life, when I hear footsteps running up the stairs. With the dress in my hands, I hide under the bed.

"Manue. Manue. It's us!" says Betta. She's breathless.

This feels like a dream.

"Get out, Manue!" she shouts.

I look under the blanket and see so many feet. Betta has thrown herself on the ground. Her face is close to mine. She's crying and laughing. For a moment she looks like Mom.

"They let us go," she says. "Get out."

I crawl out, Mom's dress still clutched in my arms. I look at the aunts, the cousins. They are pale. So scared that they can't open their mouths.

Betta tells me how things went. "They only kept Uncle Cesare. They locked us in a room for a long time. At one point they told us to go and get our coats. I mean, they let us go. Maybe they regretted it."

Uncle Cesare was at the Fantino, the restaurant where he sometimes meets with his friends, when the fascists raided it. Some escaped, some hid. My uncle, on the other hand, was caught. The fascists asked him where he lived and he replied, "In Via della Reginella."

"Let's go there," they said.

And so he took them home.

We'll never know why they detained only him, letting the rest of the family go. Uncle, like Mom, will end up in Germany.

Fantino's people did the spying. They say it was Celeste, the Star of the Port, who deals with both fascists and the Germans. They say she's a sellout.

I find that hard to believe. She seems like a nice girl. I think they talk like that out of envy because she's beautiful.

I've known her forever. She lives almost in front of our house. Sometimes, when she looks out of the window, I can see her. She's not capable of such a terrible thing. They only say things for revenge because none of her relatives were caught in the raid on October 16.

"Doesn't it seem strange to you?" Attilio asked me one day. "Can it be possible that none of her family was caught? Think twice."

CHAPTER FOURTEEN

Time passes and the days all seem the same to me.

I get up at three in the morning and go to Termini to sell souvenirs to soldiers. Or I go around Via Trionfale with the little cart. I sell shards and rags or I buy used stuff to resell for a profit.

I talk to Germans. They are the main source of income for the simple reason that they have money and can buy.

One day, in San Paolo, an incredible thing happens to me. I sell a wallet, a comb, some elastic, and little else for fifty lire (which is already a lot of money) to a soldier I had never seen before. He looks like a colossus. And the guy, instead of giving me fifty lire, pulls out a piece of paper so big that I almost don't recognize it. Five hundred lire! I've never seen five hundred lire!

He takes the bag with the goods and leaves.

I look at the paper. Hold it out. Bring it closer to my eyes.

It doesn't seem possible. I hold it up to the light to check if it's fake.

It could be fake with all the crooks going around these days.

It's real money!

My heart gallops in my chest. I pocket the banknote and see if there's anyone who might have seen what just happened and is waiting for me to turn my back and steal this bit of luck that's come my way.

There are people around, yes. But everyone is busy with his own business.

I put the money in the bottom of my pocket. Close it with a pin. Take the cart and walk away as if nothing had happened. I even find myself humming, "Vieni, c'è una strada nel bosco, il suo nome conosco, vuoi conoscerlo tu."

After turning the corner and checking that neither the German colossus nor any ill-intentioned people are following me, off I go! I run like a ferret, without paying attention to the shards bumping into each other and threatening to break. I run as I have never run in my life.

But I don't go home immediately. Better to avoid the German or some delinquent who has seen my treasure. If he follows, I don't want him to know where I live. So I go around Trastevere. Walk as far as Borgo before I decide to take the road to the ghetto.

When I get to Via della Reginella, I am so soaked with sweat it looks like I've fallen into a fountain with all my rags. I go straight to our room, where Dad continues pining for Mom.

"Here," I tell him, handing him the banknote.

He gives me an ugly look. "Where did you get this?" he asks in the terrible voice from when he was stern and we were all afraid of him. "You didn't steal it, did you?"

"Where would I get it?" I ask, replying for the first time in a man's voice that neither he nor I recognize.

"Where did you get it?" He gets out of bed. Comes close to me.

I tell him what happened. I tell him about the German colossus I've never seen before. "He's new. Maybe he just arrived and doesn't understand the value of our money."

"Maybe," he says, straightening his back.

Suddenly he seems alive again. His eyes are alive. His curiosity drives him to speak. He wants to know. His voice is alive and no longer seems to come out of the bottom of a cave.

Betta, who has just entered the room, looks at us astonished.

He signals for her to close the door, then, when he is a step away from us he says, "No one must know anything of this. People would kill for less than this." He lifts the banknote with a trembling hand.

Betta and I nod our heads in agreement. No one will know anything.

We are delighted, you know! The two of us are doing great. But if Daddy goes back to being a father of the family, everything would be much better.

And while we're waiting for Mom's return, we'll start preparing an unforgettable party for her. We'll use part of this money.

Dad goes to the wardrobe. Pulls out a clean shirt. A pair of almost-new trousers. Looks for the hat he wears when he wants to make a good impression. He asks Betta if she could please bring him the tub and a jug full of water.

Suddenly it is as if the veil of death that's enveloped him since he found out about Ginotta has fallen away. But this change doesn't depend on money, no. The amazing news was like an earthquake that woke him up from his daze and brought him back to us.

I'm not going to San Paolo for a week. I'm too afraid of meeting the colossus. Instead, I hang out in the Monti district. In Via Trionfale. In Trastevere. I go back and forth along the Viale dei Re. When I arrive at San Pietro, I stand under the Colonnade to sell keyrings and souvenirs to Catholic foreigners who want a souvenir of Rome.

Then, because San Paolo is a good place to sell my things, I decide to go back there.

I go there, yes.

And you think I don't meet him?

Yeah! He's the first one I see!

My blood freezes. I can't turn back because he's signaling for me to come closer.

What do I do now?

If I run, it will be worse. He has the machine gun at hand and with one blast he'll knock me out.

So?

So I get closer, smiling real nice. And if he asks me about the five hundred lire? I will improvise.

I struggle to push the cart. It seems to be loaded with lead. Smiling, I reach him. He smiles too, and instead of grabbing me by the shirt and asking me about the money, he rummages through the shards to find something he likes. He picks up a glass with a gold rim.

"It's very nice," he says. He opens his wallet and gives me ten lire.

I am so confused that, for a moment, I don't know what to do. Then I lower my head and look in the coin box for the change to give him.

"It's all right," he says. He speaks Italian better than all his fellow countrymen. "Come with me." He takes me to the bar and offers me some chocolate.

I go back to the cart. I don't understand. Not only did he not ask for his money back, but he gave me more. How come?

There could be many explanations. He's rich and doesn't care about money. Or I remind him of a brother, a son, a friend, someone he loves. Or he's a good man, someone who wants to patch up Hitler's atrocities as far as he can. A drop in the ocean, of course, but still a drop of good.

Mario, the ticket collector, comes to mind. He said that if each one of us, in our own small way, can do something, we must do it.

Mario saved me from the Germans.

This colossus has saved me from misery.

CHAPTER FIFTEEN

Now that Dad is back at work, I no longer kill myself anymore. Sometimes, when I get back to the ghetto before noon, I play with my friends. After all, I'm only twelve years old and I like playing with them. I forget about the war. About Italy suffering. I even forget about Mom who is in Germany and the party Betta and I are secretly preparing for when she returns.

I'm in the square when Attilio appears. I haven't seen him for so long, I run to meet him.

"How are you?" he asks. But you can tell that he says it just to say it. His head is somewhere else.

"If the Allies have arrived, we'd be better off," I say, parroting the words that are on everyone's lips these days. "The thing is, they really don't seem to want to hurry up!"

"They don't seem to want to hurry up?" Attilio repeats. He's furious, looking at me as if he wants to incinerate me. "Do you know where the Allies are?

Do you know where they are fighting? Do you know what carnage they are a part of?" He's raising his voice louder and louder.

I shake my head no and he, thankfully, calms down.

"Do you know what the Gustav Line is?"

I shake my head again.

"It is an armed line in the narrowest part of Italy. It goes from the Tyrrhenian Sea—the one at Ostia, where you sometimes go to splash around—to the Adriatic Sea. From Gaeta to Ortona, which is in Abruzzo. Do you understand?"

"Yes." I'm not convincing when I answer. The geography is not too clear to me. I went to school until third grade. I learned only what I need to live: reading, writing, and arithmetic.

So, he drags me by the arm to the pavement. Takes a piece of paper and a pencil from the folder. Says to me, "Pay attention!"

He draws two lines from top to bottom with a space in the middle. On the left he writes Tyrrhenian. On the right, Adriatic. Then he draws a line up a bit, goes over it with the pencil until it turns black.

"This is the Gustav Line," he says, "which goes from the Garigliano River, near Gaeta, to Ortona. This, instead," and he draws a big point a little farther down, "is Monte Cassino. It's right here, you see, that Americans, British, and Canadians are dying to come and liberate us. Here!" He draws a circle around Monte Cassino. "They're fighting what the Germans call the War of the Centimeter. Do you know what that means?"

"No."

"That they're defending every centimeter of land from the advancing of the enemy. Every centimeter, you understand? And you tell me that those people aren't hurrying to get here! Do you know how many of them are dying? Do you know?" He shouts through clenched teeth.

I don't answer.

"Do you know what the Germans say?"

Again, I don't answer.

"That all roads lead to Rome. It's true. But all the roads to Rome are mined. Do you know what that means? Do you remember the bombs in San Lorenzo? Do you remember the bodies covered in blood?"

"Enough!" I stand up. "I don't want to hear any more."

He looks at me. He gets a wrinkle in the middle of his forehead. He's thinking that I am an ignorant brat who will never become a man, I tell him.

He doesn't answer me. He crumples up the paper, throws it into the folder, puts down the pencil. His anger has subsided. He says that perhaps I am right not to want to know. To remain an ignorant brat. He listens to Radio London and is a friend of those in the Resistance. He has so much pain inside him that sometimes he feels like going mad.

"Thank goodness you have your mother!" I say to him. "Otherwise, you would already be dead."

His face grows red. He lowers his eyes. "I'm sorry, Manue," he says, murmuring. "I'm such a fool."

I go back to play with the boys to nizza e bastone, with the ammazza fionna. Attilio watches us.

I don't care what Attilio is thinking.

I play and it seems that life is the same as before. Mom is at the Singer. Or cleaning vegetables. Boiling potatoes. Knitting a scarf or a jumper. Collecting, one by one, the seven lire we need to go to the cinema.

When I look up again, Attilio is no longer standing there.

At lunchtime, my friends' mothers lean out of the windows and call, "Mama's boy, come upstairs, it's ready."

They leave the game and run home.

No one says to me, "Bello de mamma, come up! It's ready."

Who knows where my mother is? Her absence is a pain in my chest and nothing makes it go away. I stay alone in the street, with a ball to kick, and the ammazza fionna to shoot at birds.

"It's called slingshot!" shouted the teacher one day, angry with those of us who didn't speak proper Italian.

I didn't pay any attention. I speak the way they speak at home. There *slingshot* doesn't mean anything and ammazza fionna is the thing I make myself with a forked branch, an elastic band, and a piece of leather where I put a stone.

I aim at the fruits of the trees, which I eat even if they are sour. I eat them because I'm hungry. Not for pleasure!

Once, while kicking the rag ball, I see Ruth looking at me. I call out to her, but she turns her back on me and runs into a doorway. I was already sad because of all the "Mama's boys" that were raining down from the windows five minutes earlier, so her disappearance made me really sad. But I told myself I shouldn't whine like a child, because I have never been a child.

I kicked the ball again and went home.

Even though Dad went back to work and stopped crying, he still thinks about Mom. I can tell by the way he looks at the sewing machine. Or her clothes in the wardrobe. Or the hairpins that were left on the drawer chest that terrible Saturday, and which Betta, when she dusts, puts back in the exact place where they were.

Every now and then, talking with the aunts, Dad recalls a fact from when he and Mom were young. Life was difficult but good. Mom is a cheerful person, who gives courage to everyone.

I also think life before was good, but I didn't know it.

It seemed sad, ugly, full of misery and hunger. Every opportunity to escape from the ghetto was good. To go to the rich neighborhoods where I filled my eyes with beauty and could get something to eat.

I didn't know happiness was having Mom by my side. Even when she scolded you because you were in trouble. Or you didn't go to school and she threatened to tell Dad. And instead, when Dad came home, she hid you under the bed until he left again.

I feel like I can hear her. "Come out, Manue." And she would hand me the plate of lunch she set aside for me.

I can't wait for her to come back.

Sometimes, in the evening after Betta has put the brothers to bed and the room is settled, we go to the square, sit by the fountain, and organize Mom's homecoming party.

We make a list of people we want to invite. Talk about the restaurant where we will take everyone. The dress that Betta will have made for her by the tailor of Campo de' Fiori. In her trade nobody beats her.

She said that for the size she will use Mom's best dress. "I already have the dress design figured out in my head. It's a dress I saw in the newspaper, with lace in the neckline."

I like it when we dream of Mom's return.

We see her appear in the kitchen and throw ourselves at her in a collective embrace that never ends. I like to think that she'll laugh. That she'll pick up Gemma and be surprised at how much she has grown. She'll throw herself on the bed and say, "Let me rest a moment. I've come such a long way and I had to walk. The trains no longer work."

"On foot from Germany?" we'll ask in amazement.

She'll answer that the trains used to bring the people to die. Those are now out of service. In order to return to their lives, people have to use their feet, and they are more than fine to.

Then I'll tell her I was saved by a tram. That I traveled all over Rome for almost three days. That the ticket collector and drivers helped me. They even gave me the half ciriòle with the omelet inside. I'll tell her they are angels that God sent to save me.

She will tell us of the rich Germans' houses, all full of paintings and antique furniture. The knickknacks that are a hundred times more luxurious than the shards I sell.

"I rented a little cart, yes," I will tell her, proud of my business.

I spend my nights dreaming of Mom's return.

In my mind I tell her, *Remember to keep healthy, Ginotta. He who has health is rich and doesn't know it. You must take care of yourself. If the masters of the house are too pretentious, find a way to take care of yourself. We, here at home, look forward to your return.* I also tell her that the Germans will lose the war soon, as soon as the Allies cross the Gustav Line.

Hang in there, Ginotta, take care.

CHAPTER SIXTEEN

Christmas has come and I go to sell postcards in front of the theater in Torre Argentina. It's not like before when I was enchanted seeing the lights. The clothes. The cars. The ladies full of jewelry.

Now I go there out of necessity to earn a little bit of money.

Once I arrive, I open the umbrella and arrange the postcards. I wait for people to come out of the theater. But everything seems to have changed for me. Even the ladies who walk arm in arm with fascist and SS leaders seem changed. It's as if they don't really want to be next to those guys. They chatter idly and laugh on command while they wish they were somewhere else.

The men seem fake. Behind the cheerful faces there are heavy thoughts and a fear. I can see it in their eyes in both the fascists and the Germans. They have lost the security that they are the wolves who thought themselves masters of the world. They growl like wolves, but only to give themselves courage. They know the situation is tragic.

One Saturday outside the synagogue, Attilio tells me that there was a bloody Christmas in Ortona. I simply nod. I really don't want to know. He understands, says, "Shabbat shalom," and joins his family, who was talking to the rabbi. None of them look happy.

The New Year comes but the Allies cannot get over the Gustav Line, Attilio says. He's taken it into his head that he has to educate me.

"You're too intelligent to remain ignorant," he says one day when we are near the Fontana delle Tartarughe.

I don't answer him. Instead, I look at the bronze turtles poised on the edge of the pool. Sometimes I get nervous seeing them one step away from the water and always unable to reach it.

"Sooner or later I'll throw them in," I tell Attilo. I don't want to change the subject. I'm just sharing my thoughts.

"The Germans continue to massacre the Allies," he says. "Monte Cassino looks like an impenetrable stronghold."

"But the Allies are bombing Rome."

"And the Germans are making disasters everywhere. They are mass murderers." He stopped talking. He knows things I don't know. He listens to the radio and talks with his friends in the Quadraro.

"Do you remember when the king arrived at Verano in a limousine, and they threw stones at him?" he asks.

Who can forget that?

"Sure. The women were shouting 'Enough war, make peace, we want peace.'" That screaming is stuck in my brain and won't go away.

"War is a slaughterhouse because of men," he says. "No one hears the women."

"The women are the mothers," I say. "People have to hear them eventually. They give life to men and women! The mothers need to be listened to."

Someone calls Attilo and he leaves.

One day I'm sitting at the Portico d'Ottavia resting in a corner when I see a crowd of fascists in the ghetto. I think they're doing a simple check, one of those they do every now and then.

Germans are too busy right now not losing the war to think about us Jews. They keep saying we are their enemies, but we don't even have a toothpick to fight them with.

I don't think the fascists are here because of a spy who wants to collect the five thousand lire bounty placed on the head of every Jewish man.

The fascists move swiftly, without giving

explanation. They catch, grab, and take away. The youngest boy is my age.

No one understands what's happening. Relatives ask, but the black shirts simply do not answer.

It's March 23, 1944. We learn an attack has been made in Via Rasella. Many Germans died. It's confusing news, contradictory. Some say twenty-eight Germans died. Others say thirty-one. Rumors circulate in the ghetto, along with the wind that raises dust, with the leaves torn from the trees.

This time they didn't take children, old men, and women. Only men and that boy who's my age. Somebody says they took them to the prison of Regina Coeli.

But why?

Because they're Jews, right?

In Regina Coeli there are prisoners who are anti-fascists, communists, who think differently from Mussolini and Hitler. They wrote their opinions in books and newspapers. There are gypsies. People who are "different."

And then there are the Jews, taken just because they are Jews.

The next day some Catholic friends go to the prison to ask for news about those who were arrested. The fascists don't speak. Neither do the Germans.

Only later we will hear about Hitler's fury when

he heard about the massacre in Via Rasella.

Hitler shouted that a reprisal was needed, one that would make the world tremble. For every dead German, he said, fifty Italians had to be killed. They were to be executed where the bomb went off. People were to be pulled out of their houses and shot immediately.

"Fifty Italians for every German killed," he repeated.

Later, we'll find out the generals decided that ten Italians were enough for every German dead. They don't want to antagonize the world, so they'll execute only those already marked: prisoners and Jews.

We'll find out that the Germans ordered secrecy so as not to alarm the Resistance groups. This would have hindered the revenge. They'll tell why after the fact, after the reprisal has been carried out.

Attilio tells me all this.

He says the numbers of soldiers killed on March 23 were thirty-one. The next day another soldier died, so the Germans needed three hundred and twenty men.

However, when the dead Jews and prisoners were counted, it turned out three hundred and thirty-five were killed.

"An extra ten for the thirty-third German, five extra by mistake," he says through clenched teeth. "The Resistance put the bomb in the cart of a garbage collector. Other bombs were thrown from the sky. They shot people."

Attilio can't add anything else. He cries angry tears and leaves.

It feels like a dead cat is in my chest. A burden. A pain. A great effort to breathe.

It feels like when you understand the end of the world is coming, and you can't do anything to stop it.

I walk around at home as if I had a fever.

Betta cuts the fingernails and toenails of the little brothers she washed in the tub. She's too busy to notice that I'm in so much pain I can hardly breathe.

I go down to the square to get some fresh air. The kids are playing with glass marbles. They don't know about the hell we are living in. They play and the world stops there, among the marbles.

"Manue, what's wrong?" asks someone behind me.

I turn around and see Elia, who is a tailor. He lost his wife and four children on October 16. He walks the streets as if he were a ghost.

I tell him about Via Rasella and Germany's revenge. He already knows, he says, and he also knows the sequel. A Catholic friend told him.

"What sequel?" I ask.

"When they found the bodies," he says.

"Did the communists find them?"

"No. Some Salesians from a nearby institute. They saw the Germans coming and going all day long. They saw them bringing people into the quarry."

"Then they heard a loud bang."

"Bombing?" I ask.

"They used just a couple of bombs around the quarry. People went to look but they couldn't get into the quarry because of all the stones. So they took another entrance and what they found..." Elia brings his hands to his face as if to hide it and bursts into sobs.

Attilio will tell me that when the Salesians entered the caves they saw piles of corpses five feet high. It was carnage. The communists left a sign saying YOU WILL BE AVENGED.

I walk through the ghetto with that dead cat. It's getting heavier and heavier.

I want to vomit the cat out.

I want to cut my flesh and pull it out.

I want to go back to being the little kid I used to be, or grow ten years older and find myself out of this cursed time.

Children play with stones now. They make little piles that they shoot with the ammazza fionna.

The war passes through them like a wind that can't hurt them.

War is this dead cat that fills my chest. My breath can't return to normal.

On March 25, around noon, a message is issued saying, "The German command has ordered that for every German killed ten communist-Badoulian criminals are to be shot. This order has already been carried out."

Again, it's Attilio who tells me.

We're in the attic of his house, listening to Radio London. We lie on the floor, our eyes on the ceiling. A spider moves in the middle a large web, all made of thin threads, a trap almost invisible for flies and other insects.

Attilio looks at the spider in a daze. He says he's not sure whether he's looking at the web, the spider, the trap, or whether he's remembering what he saw in the common graves where he, along with the communists, went.

Suddenly he gets up, rummages through a pile of stuff piled up in a corner, and pulls out a pair of trousers. From the ankle to the knee, all the way to the waistband, they are stained with blood.

"They will be avenged," he says, murmuring.

He takes a crooked umbrella and pounds the spider web angrily. He seems to go mad.

The spider falls to the ground and runs toward the wall. But Attilio is quicker. He stomps on it and crushes, crushes with so much force, it seems he wants to break through the floor.

CHAPTER SEVENTEEN

Rome is like a wound when it becomes infected.

It's a swollen pustule of hatred and violence.

Not a day goes by that there aren't attacks. Germans and fascists dead, civilians killed like flies.

The Allies stopped around Anzio, the Allies stationed at the Gustav Line, the bread missing. After Via Rasella, the Germans reduced our food portions from one hundred and fifty to one hundred grams per person.

People are dying of hunger. Children cry. Mothers despair and scream. They protest and act like madwomen, says Attilio, who has become the news bulletin.

I, however, find myself in another world that gets the dead cat off my chest and prevents the painful news from hurting me.

Ruth has finally smiled at me. She told me, "I didn't know you have such beautiful eyes."

I got confused and must have turned the color of fire because she smiled again and asked me if it was true about the tram.

"How did you stay there for three days?" she asked. Then I told her that, if she had a minute, I could tell her.

She looked up at the window of her house, saw her mother looking at us, and said, "Not today, but tomorrow, if you want. We can meet in Argentina and you can tell me then."

Now I am in Argentina, waiting for her.

This morning, instead of going to Termini to sell souvenirs, I went to the fountain in front of the Bocca della Verità. I slipped into it and washed myself like I've never washed before. I brought with me a piece of soap and I rubbed my knees and elbows, as Mom recommended. That's where you get scabs if you don't wash well.

I soaped my hair and face so much that my eyes burned, but I didn't care. I had a towel in the cart that was so patched no one wanted to buy it, plus clean shorts, and a shirt. I splashed around in the fountain while everyone slept.

At one point I saw a group of Germans approaching. I went underwater and stayed there until I felt my lungs might burst. Then I pulled my nose out for some air and back down again. I couldn't run the risk of being taken to the security room because I was bathing. That had happened before in this same fountain.

Finally, they left and I got out. I dried and dressed. Then I went back home, leaving the cart and taking a fistful of coins. Then I headed to Torre Argentina.

I'm here waiting for her.

I like her a lot, but I don't know if she likes me.

She's not come and it's long past ten o'clock. She's mocked me and I almost regret being so perfumed, so clean. My heart beats in my chest anytime I see a girl who looks a little like her.

Like that one there, for example. That can't be her because she has a white dress on that looks like it just came out of the shop. Her family's not exactly rolling in money and...

That's her!

My heart jumps into my throat with happiness.

She's all perfumed, too, and this dress makes her look like the daughter of a gentleman.

She approaches me, smiles, looks at me in amazement. "You are so handsome," she says as if she doesn't believe it.

"Do you want chocolate?" I ask her.

She nods yes.

We go and sit in a café. I have twenty lire in my pocket. I put it aside in case of need. And this is a case of necessity because I care about her so much. If she says she'll be my friend, life will become lighter, easier. It's love that makes this magic.

We sit at a secluded table. When the waiter sees me, he winks. He knows me and knows I come here to sell shards, to buy rags and secondhand goods. He approaches to ask what we want.

Ruth says she wants a piece of chocolate.

"We do ice cream too," says the waiter.

She's surprised. We're at war. There's no milk, no sugar, no bread, no meat. How can there be ice cream?

She looks at me as if the waiter is making fun of us.

I lower my head. "He means they make chocolate ice cream. I don't know what they put in it. I haven't tasted it. But yes, let's have ice cream."

I'm so proud that my heart feels like it's bursting. She looks at me admiringly.

"Two ice creams," I say to the waiter.

I know they'll cost a fortune, but sometimes you need to catch happiness, even if it costs you twenty lire. Or fifty. Who knows?

Now that I'm alone with her at this table, in a beautiful place, with music in the background, I feel happiness. I feel like one of those gentlemen at Christmas who come out of the theater. He's well-dressed and laughing, walking around as if there was no war. I feel as if I was born today in this other world of happiness.

Ruth eats her ice cream little by little, with the tip of the spoon. I want to tell her she needs to hurry, or the ice cream will melt. But I don't want to give her the impression I'm a little boss who scolds. Also I'm not even tasting mine, excited as I am.

She finally speaks. "Did you really spend three days on the Circular?"

"Two and a half," I say.

"Always there? Without ever getting off?"

"Just to relieve myself."

"And then?"

I tell her about the ticket collectors, the drivers, the people, the depot, the cirióle with the omelet inside.

Time passes. I don't know what time it is. She's wearing the white dress. Her hair is in braids with white ribbons at the ends. She's thin, like everyone these days. She has a small mouth, a beautiful nose, eyes the color of chestnuts.

I was afraid she would ask me about Mom. About the Germans. About the truck. About how I got down there. But she knows that's the painful part. She wants to know the adventurous part, and I tell, and it seems to me that the tram becomes a fabulous place. The days spent there are part of a movie. One of those we used to go to see with Mom when she still lived with us.

My ice cream has all melted and she has finished hers.

"Do you want some?" I ask her.

"And what about you?"

"I don't feel like it."

I hand her the little cup. She sinks her spoon into the dark cream, then brings it closer to my mouth. One teaspoon for me, one for her, like this until the ice cream is gone.

"Will I see you again?" I ask her.

"Of course," she answers. "But there's no need for ice cream. We can meet in the square, at the market."

My heart dances in my chest.

"Do you still want to know about the tram?" I'm worried because the tram story will end sooner or later and I want to talk to her for a hundred years.

"Yes. But also about other things. About what you want."

The dead cat I had inside is no more.

Now there's a sea of hope. The war will end. Mom will return. I'll work and earn lots of money. And the future will be full of roses without thorns.

CHAPTER EIGHTEEN

Rome is increasingly dangerous. Fascists and Germans are more and more evil. The partisans continue to make attacks. The Allies bombing. In the streets, among the poor, fights break out over a potato or a piece of bread. Fists fly. The police arrive and bullets fly. There is no safe street.

Attilio tells me all this. He calls me to his house. We sit in the attic, and he tells me what's happening.

My head's a bit in the air. I think of Ruth and I'm happy. The fact that I can see her almost every day lights up a happiness in my heart that makes me endure every effort and forget that there is a war.

I keep my hunger. I save every cent so I can take her to that café again. Yesterday she told me she felt guilty about the ice cream we ate.

I tell her we must live life every day as if it were our last day.

"Suppose a bomb is thrown tomorrow and we all

get blown up? Suppose there's a new raid and they take us to Germany. Suppose the Allies are defeated and the Germans become the masters of Rome?"

She shakes her head no: no raid, no defeat, no nothing. "It cannot happen," she says. "The pope is in Rome."

"Big deal! He doesn't lift a finger for the Jews."

We were silent.

"Let's change the subject," she said.

"All right. But don't be sad about the ice cream."

She looks down, unconvinced.

"Next time let's bring some chocolate to your brothers and mine."

She looks at me like I'm talking nonsense.

"In my house," I say, "I'm the head of the family."

Actually it's not like that anymore but I want to make a good impression. "I bring home what's needed. If I have a few lire left, I put it aside for necessities."

"Chocolate is not a necessity."

"It's a little bit of contentment amid so much tragedy. A kind of medicine for the heart. If the heart is content," I hurry to explain, "the whole body is fine. Do you know the proverb about health?"

"No."

"'Who is healthy is rich and does not know it.' That's what my mom used to say."

Attilio takes me by the arm and shakes me out of my daydream. "Did you understand what I said?"

I turn back to him. To his talk. "No, I must confess."

"Two days ago, something terrible happened," he murmurs. "I bet you don't know anything about it."

No, I don't, and I wish he wouldn't tell me. I don't want him to put the dead cat in my chest again.

He, however, is already telling about the women who raided the bakery near the Iron Bridge. A protest that took place. It was on April 7.

"They were almost all mothers. They had their children with them. There were men, too, but more women. And they were the angriest. They knew in that bakery there was not only the bread, but also a storehouse where they kept white flour. The best kind. More than just black bread! At the Tesei bakery they make bread for the German troops stationed in Rome." He says it as if he's reading a newspaper.

I don't want to know.

"The owner of the bakery, when he saw all the crowd, was touched. He distributed bread and flour. Someone, however, was kind enough to inform the police. And of course they came rushing in immediately! They blocked the bridge on both sides, then they jumped on the people.

"Amid the confusion of those running and

shouting and kids crying and so on, the soldiers grabbed ten women at random. They lined them up on the bridge, facing the river. They fired bursts of machine-gun shots, killing them all without thinking twice."

He says it quickly as if he knew that interrupting himself, he wouldn't be able to continue.

My tongue is stuck to the roof of my mouth.

I seem to see the scene. The women protesting for bread. The soldiers arriving to take back the bread that could fill them. The people running away. The women being caught. The bursts of machine-gun fire that brought them to the ground.

"They were mothers who could no longer bear to hear their children crying from hunger," Attilio says.

The bitterness of the chocolate comes back into my mouth. Ruth is right to feel guilty about the ice cream. People die for a loaf of bread, for a handful of flour to take home, and we indulge.

"I knew one of them," Attilio says. "I went to the Iron Bridge. The bodies were still there, among the loaves of bread and the flour stained with blood. There was a priest who was blessing them."

Attilio lies on the ground, his hands on the back of his neck, his eyes on the ceiling.

I'm standing, my back against the wall. He's so skinny that it's scary. There are black circles under his eyes. His nose looks longer. He has such a great anger that I worry he'll end up doing something reckless.

I would tell him to be careful, not to get into trouble, that if they arrest him, it will be horrible. The idea of him ending up in Via Tasso to be tortured gives me goose bumps.

But he's talking again. He says in Rome it's not just the bread that is lacking. It's also exasperation, hatred, fear, all together—these things are a vapor that rises in the air. And sooner or later it explodes.

"The constant arrests," he says. "They arrest you for nothing. For no reason. Not just because you're Jewish or a communist. Do you know why they arrest you?" he asks, turning to me. "Because they need a workforce."

"In Germany?"

"Even here in Rome. There is a need for labor to clear away the rubble from the bombings. To repair trains and trams. To shore up crumbling buildings. Who do you think could do those jobs? The Germans? Of course not!" He laughs, nibbling the nail of his index finger. He pulls at the skin and a line of blood appears on his finger.

I think of Mom. Of when she pricked herself with the pin. I can't think of blood anymore.

"Who does those jobs?" I ask him this just to make him happy.

"Prisoners."

We look at each other. I wish he would stop.

He keeps talking. There's no mercy for my age or my longing for a moment of peace amid this tragedy.

"The Germans fill the prisons as if they were a storehouse for the workforce. Then they sort the men where they are needed. You here, you there, you over there. And if you die, what does it matter? Sooner or later you have to die anyway!" He laughs in an ugly way. I don't like it.

"The wives, who know this, go to see their husbands under the windows of the prison. They wait for them to come out. They talk to them. They tell them that the children are well, that they are well. They tell them lies, because this isn't the truth. But lies are needed when a husband is in prison. Everyone needs them. Even throwing a piece of bread at your husband is useful because in prison, you're not in the Grand Hotel. They don't feed you! They throw the pieces of bread from the street to the window. Like Teresa did, you know?"

"Who?"

He devours me with his eyes. "Gullace!" he almost shouts. "Don't tell me you haven't heard."

"The Calabrian woman murdered under Regina Coeli?"

"Yes, her."

"I didn't know her name was Teresa," I say.

As long as the dead have no face, no name, no history, they go into the sea of dead and you don't pay attention. But when they come to you and tell you their name, who they are, what they did, why they died, then it is like an extra wound in your heart.

"She was pregnant," he says. "She was holding her eldest son. She kept throwing bread toward her husband's cell. Her husband told her to stop. To go home. She kept doing it. A German arrived. He told her to leave. She tried to throw the bread one last time. He shot her. She had six more children at home."

"Enough," I say, my voice low.

He's furious. "Enough? Are you a fool? These things must be known! These things must remain in everyone's memory so that it doesn't happen again. Do you understand? These are terrible facts. We cannot close our eyes and plug our ears! Grow up, Manue. Become a man for real! That's what life is, even if it horrible!"

My head spins. My ears ring. I feel like I'm going to fall over at any moment.

He keeps talking. He says a lot of people went where Teresa's body was and filled the area with flowers."

"It will become the symbol of the Resistance," he says. "The Germans don't have much longer. I hope what happened in Naples, where the citizens said 'Enough!' and the Germans had to flee, happens here."

"Is it happening here?" I want to forget Teresa Gullace being murdered in front of her son.

"Not long now," he says, but he doesn't seem convinced.

I know what he's thinking. The pope is in Rome. The anger is extinguished by promising paradise.

I tell myself that it's better they took Mom to Germany. She's much safer there.

CHAPTER NINETEEN

And then comes the joy!

It comes early one morning. It catches me in my sleep. It comes along with someone shouting, "The Allies have arrived! They are here! They have arrived!"

I run to the window.

It's Celeste, the Star of the Port. She's telling everyone the great news. Her voice is drenched with joy as she shouts that the Allies have arrived. That the war is over. Finally over!

Balconies and windows open. Here on Via della Reginella we can't believe it. "Really? Is that possible?"

Doors open. People come out into the street.

"They have arrived! Yes, it's all true!" Celeste keeps shouting. She is so full of happiness that she looks even more beautiful.

From the other windows people are insulting her.

"Spy!" they call her. "Sellout."

Bad things are being said. Very bad.

She looks around bewildered.

Everything people wouldn't say while Germans and fascists were the masters, they now vomit up on her with so much rage she closes the window and shuts herself indoors.

But what does it matter, Celeste? The swearing and the insults?

"They have arrived. They have finally arrived," I shout it all around home. Uncles and cousins wake up, they don't understand.

"The Allies," I say. "They're here. They are in Rome!"

In a flash, I go out into the street. The people seem drunk. They come out of the houses like when you get out of a prison and the sun dazzles you. You look around and you don't understand.

I see faces that have been gone for months. Men I thought were swallowed up by bombed trains, by prisons, or by the Tevere. I see people who seem to have survived a long winter underground.

From the Portico d'Ottavia, I run toward the Marcellus Theatre. From there toward Piazza Venezia.

There are jeeps, trucks, and vans in the streets loaded with everything. Even beer, they tell me.

Soldiers laughing. Throwing cigarettes and cartons of chocolate.

Applause starts from the streets. There's applause everywhere. There's a happiness. Euphoria. It's impossible to say.

Free at last.

Free.

And safe!

No more planes bombing us from the sky. No more roundups. No more jails, interrogations, torture. No more bombings, bridges being blown up, women killed for a piece of bread. No more orphans and widows, dead bodies in common graves by the roadside. Nothing of nothing and everything of everything.

People hug each other. Adults and children. Old men with trembling hands and eyes full of tears.

"Why are you crying?" I ask a man.

He doesn't answer me. He can't. He just makes the sign of the cross and shakes the hand of a little girl who calls him grandfather.

I look for Attilio, but I don't see him. There are too many people, too much crowd, too many horns, whistles, and applause. More applause.

A man with a trumpet leans out of the window and plays so loud that his lungs might burst.

The people are a compact sea, dense like the one that opened up in front of Moses and the people fleeing from Egypt. Except in the middle of this sea of people, it's not Moses and the Jews passing through, but the caravan of liberators.

Hurray for the liberators!

"It's the Fifth Army," says someone standing next to me. "The Americans did it before the British. There was a competition to see who could enter Rome first!"

Americans. British. Who cares?

I throw myself into the sea of people. Let myself be carried by the crowd to the balcony where the duce, with his chest out, his hands on his hips, his ugly mug, and his iron voice, was making speeches about Judaism as fascism's irreconcilable enemy.

He forbade us Jews the right to study, to marry Aryans, to work.

He declared war against the plutocratic and reactionary democracies of the West.

I feel like I can still hear his evil voice in my ears. The roar of the crowd in delirium at every catchphrase that came out of his mouth.

Now the balcony is empty.

The square is crowded with delirious people. But not for him, whose days are numbered. Delirium for the liberators, for these cheerful young men who fill the air with songs and candy, chewing gum, cigarettes, and kisses, who join the applause of the people, drunk with happiness.

I look back at the balcony and I have a gut feeling.

Something swells under my sternum and beats, beats like a bitter heart. Something was left in a cage of brooding pain, resentment, and now it wants to see the light.

The scream comes choking out of my mouth. "I'm Jewish. I'm Jewishhhh!"

I scream loud, louder, and the voice becomes clear, very clear. "I'm Jewishhhh!" I raise my hand toward that balcony. Beat at the air.

"I'm Jewish!" I laugh and feel like crying. Then I laugh and cry, laugh and cry at the same time. There are so many around me who have the joy of someone born again stamped on their faces.

You see, Ginotta, I say in my mind to Mom. *You do you see that the time for liberation has come? Soon you will come home.*

We no longer must hide.

We no longer must live underground like the dead, or in caves, or in cellars, or on the street with false documents that save us up to a certain point. Or on the street without papers with the terror of being caught and taken away.

This is what freedom is, Ginotta. This!

I put two fingers in my mouth and let out a high-pitched whistle.

A blond soldier turns towards me. He raises his arms, his fingers the "V" of victory. Then he leans towards a sack, fills his cupped hands with sweets, throws them in the air.

Candy like colorful confetti rains down on me, again and again. The kids around me compete to pick it up.

I stand under this rainbow shower, enjoying the end of a nightmare from which I thought I would never wake up.

CHAPTER TWENTY

And then there's the aftermath.

It's the tail of the nightmare. That which becomes a reality and that I'll have to live with for the rest of my life.

We planned a beautiful party for Mom. We thought of everything. The relatives to invite. What to eat. The music and the songs to sing because in the celebrations of return, one cannot help but sing. Even in the Bible it's written, "When the Lord brought back the captives of Zion, we thought we were dreaming. Then our mouth was opened to a smile, our tongues melted into songs of joy."

I looked forward to seeing her arrive. I wanted to run to her and hold her. Tell her how hard life was without her. Hard and sad. Full of an effort that I didn't feel before even if I was struggling a hundred times over.

She would have given me a tight hug for sure.

She would have said that I was an exaggerator. That life is always a struggle but not a tragedy! Of the 1,023 people that the Germans took away on October 16, only 16 came back. Fifteen men and Settimia Spizzichino.

That day in 1945, when we were told that the survivors of the extermination camps (more than just labor camps!) were coming back, I lurked at the window.

I hoped with all my might that Mom would appear. That she would hurry up.

Come on, Ginotta, come on. Run!

I looked from one side of the street to the other.

Waiting, always waiting.

But the hours passed and she didn't show up.

I stood there from morning till night, my eyes burning and my heart too. I didn't want to give up. I kept hoping. The others had made it, why not her? I kept talking to her in my mind, *Come on, Ginotta, courage. It's not long now.*

"Maybe tomorrow," said Betta, who occasionally came close to me.

I didn't sleep that night. I strained my ears, hoping to hear her footsteps stopping in front of the door. If I heard footsteps approaching the doorway, I would fly to the window, but it was always someone else.

She didn't come the next day.

We kept waiting, burning our eyes with watching. Then, unable to resist, we went to see Settimia.

There was a bunch of people in front of her house. Everyone was asking, questioning, looking for hope.

When it was our turn, she looked at us. She shook her head. "Not two hours after we were in Birkenau, they sent her to the gas chambers."

We returned home in silence.

I threw myself on the bed. My legs couldn't hold me up.

Neither could my heart. It was as if I had lost the center of life.

I wanted to cry and scream, to call out to her until she appeared. I wanted to turn back the clock by two years and stop her from going to Termini. She would have survived. Our family was not on the list. We (for some mistake or carelessness) had not been sentenced to death. And at Termini the raid would not have been carried out, so Dad would have survived too.

You went in Jonàv's mouth! I'm saying it in my mind. I say it angrily and sadly the same as she said it to me that Saturday when the German had thrown me on the truck.

Why, Ginotta, why? I clench my fists, clench my teeth until they grind. I want to smash everything but I don't even have the strength to get up.

With the sheet pulled over my face, I feel like sinking into the huge hole in my heart. Once hope was planted there but that's been torn away by a murderer's hand. What would I have done without her?

Who would have said to me, "Manue, take care of yourself, don't get into trouble?" Who would have loved me as only a mother can love you?

A big hole in the heart. A pain that can't find peace.

I went through the streets pushing the cart and I didn't have the strength to shout. Women would appear, give me things in exchange for others, they bought things, putting the right money in my hands. I had lost my voice and enthusiasm.

What I was doing? The life I was living, all of it, no longer excited me.

Then, one day, I dreamt of her. She was next to me, looking at me, saying to me, "Manue, God gives and God takes away. Didn't I teach you that this is how it is?" She said life goes on. What did I want? A tragedy? "No, Manue, no tragedy. We don't like tragedies. We never have."

CHAPTER TWENTY-ONE

I am ninety-one years old and this morning, like almost every day, I am on the tram. I like to get around Rome, either on foot or by public transportation. If I'm tired of waiting, I grab a taxi and get a ride home.

When I think of the past, I tell myself that in the midst of so many death trains that brought Jews to their death, there was a tram that brought a twelve-year-old boy toward life.

I hold my mother in my heart as a great love. In my memory, she remained young, thirty-seven years old. Younger than my son's daughter, who is forty-three.

We went to the concentration camp where she died by gassing. There were about fifty of us. We flew to Krakow and from there we drove by bus. We went to Auschwitz-Birkenau. It was the month of June. We had coats because it was cold.

"We are in the most efficient Nazi extermination camp," the guide told us. "Here they died in gas chambers, by lethal injection, hangings, shootings, by being tortured, or from starvation. There were more than four million individuals, almost all Jews."

Auschwitz is made up of several camp complexes, one of the largest being Birkenau. We walked a lot. Many people who were younger than me stopped. They couldn't make it. I, on the other hand, managed to walk through it all.

There was a silence that gave me goose bumps more than the cold. An absolute silence.

Everyone thought of his dead. Everyone walked as though in a funeral procession. Death was there in every centimeter of ground, in every breath of air we breathed.

When we reached the tenements, many of the women in the group felt sick. There were rooms full of hair, of suitcases, of glasses, of children's shoes.

They made a museum there.

I was trying to understand what Mom saw, where her eyes had rested, if she had understood they were sending her to die. Or did she really think they were taking her to the showers to clean herself up after that terrible journey. I think it was better that she died immediately, so she didn't suffer what the others suffered.

At one point, the guide told us this was the camp where the prisoners of the ghetto of Rome had been taken, those who came on October 16.

Then Gemma, my only sister who remained, said to me, "This is where Mom died."

The rabbi heard her, interrupted the guide's explanations. "Let us recite a psalm for Virginia Piazza," he murmured.

We recited the psalm, and thus we bid her farewell for good.

I thought of her again.

Her hands, her voice, the cacio e pepe she prepared like no one else. The raindrops that shone in her hair, like so many small fires. The morning she looked out her window and saw the Germans. She looked beautiful. She remained beautiful inside of me. No one in the world loved me as much as she did.

As I ride the tram to Torre Argentina, a memory comes to me of when I was little. I had a lira, a nickel coin. I was playing near the door of my house, equipped with a large lock, which opened with a large iron key. I slipped the penny into the lock, and I couldn't pick it up again. Thank goodness that the key turned anyway, otherwise I would have received a reprimand, both for the lost lira and for the trouble with the lock.

Time has passed and I have forgotten about

that fact. A few years ago, thieves attempted to rob the house by picking the lock. They couldn't get in because, in the meantime, I arrived. They heard my footsteps on the stairs and ran, passing me before I realized the situation.

I called the locksmith to have the lock changed, which was too old by then, and if the thieves came back, they would have no problem getting in and taking everything away.

That's when I found the coin. It had been locked in there for more than seventy years.

I was a kid again. Mom was working at the Singer. Grandfather was hanging a beef salami from the hooks in the ceiling. The sun came in through the window.

It's a beautiful day. I'm thinking of the lira that fell in the lock. It's well-preserved, in case of need I can always get it back.

Mom has remained in my heart like that coin in the lock. The thing is, no one is coming to pick my heart.

Mom stays here, inside me.

Forever.

ABOUT THE AUTHOR

Tea Ranno was born in Melilli, in the province of Syracuse, in 1963, and has lived in Rome since 1995. She has a degree in law and deals with law and literature. She has published for and/or the novels *Cenere* (2006, finalist for the Calvino and Berto awards, winner of the Chianti award) and *In una lingua che non so più dire* (2007). In 2012, Mondadori released *La sposa vermiglia* and in 2014, again for Mondadori, *Viola Fòscari*. In 2018 for Frassinelli she released *Sentimi* and in 2019 for Mondadori *L'amurusanza*.